The Book of Isaiah

The Book of ISAIAH

A NEW TRANSLATION · WITH DRAWINGS BY CHAIM GROSS

INTRODUCTION BY H. L. GINSBERG

THE JEWISH PUBLICATION SOCIETY OF AMERICA

PHILADELPHIA · 5733 · 1973

COPYRIGHT © 1972

BY THE JEWISH PUBLICATION SOCIETY OF AMERICA

FIRST EDITION

ALL RIGHTS RESERVED

ISBN 0-8276-0005-4

LIBRARY OF CONGRESS CATALOG CARD NUMBER 78-188581

MANUFACTURED IN THE UNITED STATES OF AMERICA

DESIGNED BY ABE LERNER

Contents

Introduction

Frank Moore Cross, Jr., writes in *The Ancient Library of Qumran and Modern Biblical Studies*, New York, 1958, p. 26: "It seems clear that the great library once housed in the . . . community center was abandoned in Cave IV. . . ." And on p. 34: "The most popular books among the sectarians, to judge from the number of copies preserved, are Deuteronomy, 14 MSS; Isaiah, 12 MSS; and Psalms, 10 MSS." Interestingly enough, the situation in Rabbinic Judaism is very similar. No book of the Torah is quoted so often as Deuteronomy, no book of the Neviim (Prophets) so often as Isaiah, and no book of the Ketuvim (Hagiographa) so often as the Psalms.

Deuteronomy, of course, is notable for its warm tone and its flowing, quotable style. The Jewish confession of faith consists of the one verse Deut. 6.4, "Hear, O Israel! The Lord is our God, the Lord alone." The *Shema* ("Hear," the first word of the verse just cited) which the adult male Jew is required to recite twice daily consists of Deut. 6.4-9; 11.13-21; Num. 15.37-41. The first of these passages is repeated again when one retires for the night. The first two passages are also contained in the *mezuzah* that is affixed to a doorpost at the entrance of a dwelling and of every room that people live in, and the same two plus Exod. 13.1-10, 11-16 in the tefillin (phylacteries) worn by men on weekdays during morning prayer (or, on fast days, other than Yom Kippur, at the afternoon prayer). As regards the Book of Psalms, it is of course the book of devotion. Some psalms and bits of psalms are recited before the morning prayers every day; some psalms are prescribed for particular days in the week or in the year; and any psalm or psalms may be recited to express a prayerful mood. The Book of Isaiah, finally, of which Qumran Cave I contained two other copies, one of which is the famous complete Isaiah scroll (referred to in the footnotes to our translation as 1QIsᵃ), has yielded more *haftaroth* than any other book in the Prophets.

Nearly half of these are accounted for by the liturgical requirement that seven *haftaroth* of consolation be read after the fast of Tish 'ah be-Ab. For as we read in Ben Sira ch. 48:

22 . . . . the prophet Isaiah,
   great and certain in his vision,

. . . .
. . . .

24 With a mighty spirit he foresaw the last things
   and comforted those who mourned in Zion;
25 he revealed the future to the end of time,
   the unknown before it occurred.

In penning the last two verses, Ben Sira of course had in mind mainly chs. 40-66, the block from which "the seven *haftaroth* of consolation" are culled. In fact, his v. 24b is obviously inspired by Isa. 61.2-3. Modern scholarship, however, does not share Ben Sira's view that all the prophecies in the *book* of Isaiah stem from the eighth century B.C.E. *prophet* Isaiah; and on the post-Isaian authorship of just chs. 40-66 (as well as on some other chapters and passages) there is virtually complete unanimity. This is therefore a convenient place for clearing up two widespread misunderstandings:

(1) that such a belief is incompatible with loyalty to Judaism, and

(2) that it is motivated by a desire to debunk or disparage.

As regards the former, the late Chief Rabbi of the British Commonwealth, J. H. Hertz, wrote in *The Pentateuch and the Haftorahs* (1956), p. 942: "The question can be considered dispassionately. It touches no dogma, or any religious principle in Judaism." And against the second misconception, one might recall how in a recent bestselling novel (Chaim Potok, *The Promise*, New York, 1969, p. 327) a candidate for the rabbinic diploma at a Brooklyn yeshiva defends, in his answers to his examiners, the historico-critical method of studying Talmud which his father, one of its distinguished exponents, has taught him: "I kept saying over and over again that I was not trying to be disrespectful to the Gemara but was only trying to better my understanding of it." It is this writer's hope that his sober striving to advance the understanding of the remarkable Book of Isaiah will be obvious, and that it will be judged to have achieved a measure of success.

The basic division of the Book of Isaiah A, comprising chs. 1-33 and 36-39, and Isaiah B, comprising chs. 34-35, 40-66.

Isaiah A (or "First Isaiah"), comprises a *Body*, consisting of chs. 1-33, and a *Historical Appendix,* consisting of chs. 36-39. The Body consists of *pronouncements and prophecies* attributed (not all of them correctly) to Isaiah son of Amoz, with no narrative frameworks except in chs. 6, 7, 8, and 20; the Historical Appendix, on the other hand, is a *narrative about* three *incidents* in the reign of Hezekiah in which Isaiah played a part and/or made prophetic utterances.

According to the superscription of the Book of Isaiah, "Isaiah son of Amoz prophesied concerning Judah and Jerusalem in the reigns of Uzziah, Jotham, Ahaz, and Hezekiah, kings of Judah." Certain other data enable us to fix the beginning and the end of his prophetic activity a little more exactly. In 6.1, Isaiah himself dates his famous throne vision "in the year that King Uzziah died." Most recent writers date the death of King Uzziah in the year 734 B.C.E.; and since most recent writers have with good reason (as will be shown) given up the old view that ch. 6 records the call of Isaiah, his activity must have begun a few years before 734, say between 740 and 735. Again, the Historical Appendix relates three episodes in which Isaiah played a part, partly at and partly near the time of Sennacherib's invasion of Judah, which is known to have taken place in the year 701; and while these stories exhibit some legendary traits, they obviously contain a susbtantial core of history, and that there was some communication between Hezekiah and Isaiah is surely a part of it. (The same, by the way, may be said of the third person narrative in 7.3 ff. about an encounter between Isaiah and Hezekiah's predecessor, Ahaz.)

Isaiah was probably born in Jerusalem; that he lived in Jerusalem is certain. Passages whose Isaian authorship is not disputed are concerned specifically with the city and its temple. In 1.21-27, he contrasts in elegiac tones what he believes to have once been the character of Jerusalem as a "faithful city filled with justice" and its shocking present state, with magistrates who will not hear the lawsuit of just those who are most in need of redress because they are apt to be too poor to pay an adequate baksheesh; the prophet goes on to predict that the Lord will purge the city of its "dross" and "will restore your judges as of yore and your counselors as aforetime." He apostrophizes Jerusalem and/or its inhabitants (or its ruling class) in 5.3 ff., 22.1 ff., and 29.1 ff. His contacts with dignitaries of Ahaz and Hezekiah are (unlike those with the sovereigns) reported by Isaiah himself, in 8.2 and 22.15 respectively. Of all the prophets, only he has occasion to refer to the waters of Siloam (Isa. 8.6; called Shelah in Neh. 3.15) and to Jerusalem's reservoirs (Isa. 22.9b, 11a), to the citadel of Jerusalem (known as "the city of David," Isa. 22.9a; cf. II Sam. 5.7, 9; etc.) and to her armory (Isa. 22.8c, on which see the footnote to the translation). When he needs a simile for the coming decimation of the population of Ephraim, he compares the ratio of the grain that the reapers harvest in the Valley of Rephaim to what remains for the gleaners (17.5). For the Valley of Rephaim, a residential section in the southwestern part of present-day Jerusalem, was only an expanse of grainfields to the west of the (according to our notions, exceedingly small) Jerusalem of Isaiah. Because Jerusalem was both a royal city and a temple city, it is sometimes named in addition to Judah as though it were not part of it but coordinate with it. Isaiah is one of those who in such cases always put Jerusalem before Judah—Isa. 3.1, 8; 5.3; 22.21—but, for example, the editor or editors who furnished the superscriptions Isa. 1.1, 2.1 employs the opposite order. Isaiah venerates Jerusalem because he venerates Jerusalem's temple. He has a vision of the Lord holding court in the temple (ch. 6), and he describes the Lord as "the LORD of Hosts who dwells on Mount Zion (8.8)." In a famous passage he tells his hearers that visiting the temple, sacrificing there, and praying there are all useless, even abhorrent to the Lord, in the absence of ethical conduct; but even there he does not deny that such visits constitute "coming to appear in My presence" and "trampling My courts" (1.12). The remarkable role he assigns to the temple for the future (2.2-4) will be discussed further on. It will be helpful to the reader of Isaiah to note that "Zion" denotes any of the following: (1) the hill whose southern spur is the site of the urban center of a non-Israelite city state (it was called Jerusalem and its inhabitants were called Jebusites) on the border between the Israelite tribes of Judah and Benjamin which was annexed by David, who made his home in the citadel ("the city of David") at the town's higher, or northern end; (2) the site above, i.e., to the north of, this spur on which Solomon built "the House of the Lord," Jerusalem's famous temple; (3) Jerusalem as a whole.

To the belief that Zion was the Lord's abode, a belief in the divine grace by which it was ruled by the dynasty that had acquired Jerusalem for Israel, had settled permanently in Jerusalem, and had built Jerusalem's temple as part of the royal palace complex, was a natural complement. Indeed, we are justified in speaking of these two doctrines as "the Jerusalem theology." These ideas are frequently expressed in the Book of Psalms, which is the songbook of the Jerusalem temple; and some of the compositions in question may very well have been in existence already in Isaiah's time. At any rate, Pss. 20, 48, and 76, which celebrate Jerusalem as "the city of God" and therefore inviolable, are not very likely to have been composed after the destruction of the city by the Babylonians in the year 586 B.C.E.; and Ps. 20, for example, which prays that in time of distress the Lord may accept the offerings (v. 4) of His anointed (v. 8)—meaning the king whose head (or perhaps only whose ancestor's head) was anointed with oil in token of consecration to the Lord—and that He may respond by appointing ("sending") help and success for him "from His sanctuary . . . from Zion" (v. 3), obviously refers to a king of the present (not an eschatological "messiah") and to a Zion of the present, and must likewise date from before 586 B.C.E. (Incidentally, "His sanctuary" in v. 3 means heaven, as proved by v. 7 and by Ps. 150.1; so that the parallelism in v. 3 makes Zion the abode of the Lord only in the sense that the temple is regarded as an extension of His heavenly abode.) Like Ps. 20, Pss. 2, 21, and 72 are content to pray for, and/or note the Lord's graciousness toward, the king who is reigning in Zion at the moment. Similarly, Ps. 144.1-11, a late abridgment of Ps. 18//II Sam. 22, has David pray and give thanks only for himself, which suggests at least the possibility that in the abridger's copy of Ps. 18//II Sam. 22, v. 51 comprised only the words "Who accords wondrous victories to His king,/Who deals graciously with His anointed!" (cf. I

Sam. 2.10b!), the line "With David and his offspring evermore" being, in that case, a secondary expansion. However, the doctrine of a divine promise of perpetual grace to the dynasty of David is enunciated in unambiguous terms in Ps. 89.4-5, 20-38 (cf. II Sam. 7.8-17), and the plight of the king who invokes this promise in vv. 39-52 has suggested to one scholar the plight of Hezekiah in II Ki. 18.13-16 and to another even that of Ahaz in II Ki. 16.5-6, either of which identifications would make the psalm contemporary with Isaiah. In any case, Isaiah's prophecies leave no doubt but that he subscribed to the doctrine. Indeed, it would seem, as more than one writer has observed, that by the middle of the eighth century B.C.E. the David-and-Zion ideology had become so firmly established at the center of the official theology of Judah that the earlier great ages in the history of salvation, the Patriarchal and the Mosaic ages, and their heroes, had been pushed to the periphery. The two eighth century Judite prophets, Amos and Isaiah, offer nothing comparable to the references to the Patriarchs and to Moses in the two eighth century Israelite prophets Deutero-Micah (i.e., Mi. chs. 6-7, which is dated by Mi. 7.14 relatively early in the reign of Jeroboam II, or ca. 780-770 B.C.E.: Israel has recovered from the Arameans what it lost in western Palestine, but Bashan and Gilead, which seem to the speaker more desirable—as much as farm land is preferable to scrub—still await liberation; see II Ki. 13.22-24; 14.23-25) and Deutero-Hosea (i.e., Hos. chs. 4-14, dating from the 740s B.C.E.). On the Patriarchs and their age, see Mi. 7.20 and Hos. 12.3-5, 13; on Moses and his age, Mi. 6.4-5 and Hos. 9.10; 12.14-13.1, 4-5. As against that, Amos and Isaiah make no mention at all of the Patriarchs and their age (except for a solitary reference to Abraham in Isa. 29.22, where, however, syntax and better logic require that *avraham* be amended to *avotam*, "Assuredly, thus said the LORD to the House of Jacob whose ancestors He redeemed: Neither shall Jacob be put to shame now, neither shall his face blanch now"), and they only refer to the bare fact of the exodus and/or the crossing of the sea or the sojourn in the wilderness and to the bare fact of the conquest: for the exodus, etc., see Am. 2.10; 3.1; 5.25; Isa. 11.16; for the conquest, Am. 2.9; Isa. 17.9—all without even an allusion to Moses or any other personality. The one great figure of the past that Amos and

Isaiah do name is David: Am. 6.5; 9.11; Isa. (apart from phrases like "the House of David," "the throne of David," etc.) 29.1, 3 (see note to the translation). In addition, Isaiah refers to two famous victories of David, though without naming him, in 28.21. (37.35 is very striking, but it occurs in a highly legendary context [see below on chs. 36-39] and so must be treated with caution.)

If as a Jerusalemite Isaiah was familiar with the Jerusalem theology and traditions, as a cultured man he was familiar with much else. The influence of his older contemporary Amos is unmistakable in two areas: (1) His social message: cult is of no use without justice. Isa. 1.10-17 obviously echoes Am. 5.21-25, and a reader can easily pick out the identical or equivalent phrases. The same applies to the outcry against injustice and oppression of the poor in Isa. 5.8-10, 23; 10.1-2, on the one hand, and in Am. 2.6b-7a; 3.15; 5.11-12, on the other. (2) His review of the calamities that failed to make Israel turn over a new leaf and his threat of a climactic catastrophe. For Isaiah's review of the history of Israel in the past couple of decades in Isa. 9.7 ff. as a continuation of Amos's earlier survey in Am. 4.6 ff., compare the note to the translation of Isa. 9.7.

Another literary influence is evident in Isa. 1.2-4: the call to heaven and earth to listen while the prophet, in the name of the Lord, denounces the Lord's faithless children is irresistibly reminiscent of Deut. 32.1 ff., and the resemblance extends to the alternation between quotation from the Lord (Isa. 1.2b-3; Deut. 32.20-35) and prophetic comment (Isa. 1.4; Deut. 32.36).

Finally, Isaiah seems to have known and been influenced by the older sections of the Book of Proverbs. For one thing, the most characteristic thing about Isaiah's theology is that he considers pride the root and essence of wickedness. (Conversely, humility is the essence of goodness; and since it is most often to be found in the poor, one almost gets the impression—probably erroneous—that indigence is itself a virtue, cf. 3.14-15; 10.1; 11.4; 14.32b; 30.2; 29.19.) Thus, idolatry, to Isaiah, is nothing but the arrogance of men who treat their own handiwork as gods. Isa. 2 begins by predicting that all the nations will come to worship the God of Jacob, but it continues (2.5-8) by noting that for the present the House of Jacob itself is not free from idolatry (2.9-21).

So it concludes that mankind will only be cured of it when the Lord so shakes the earth that everything tall and proud is toppled; then man, in terror of the dread majesty of the Lord, will flee into the caves and hollows of the earth and, realizing his own insignificance, will cast his idols to the bats that inhabit such places. Even the coquettish finery of the ladies of Jerusalem is offensive because it is a manifestation of pride, 3.16 ff. So of course what makes the "fat cats" of Jerusalem prefer banqueting to brooding over Isaiah's Cassandra-like warnings is conceit (5.11-21, especially vv. 15-16, 21). And what other explanation can there be for the disregard, in the sister kingdom of Ephraim, of the warning of previous setbacks (9.7-9)? And what makes Assyria so cruel? The answer to this is given in 10.7-15; for a quick orientation see v. 12. What is characteristic of Isaiah are of course the pervasiveness of this idea and the insistence with which it is applied. Now, there are some parallels in Psalms which may antedate Isaiah: Ps. 31.19, 24; 36.12, and perhaps 94.2; 140.6. But a much more important factor in the evolution of Isaiah's doctrine is probably the pointed identification of evil with arrogance by personified Wisdom in Prov. 8.13: "To revere the LORD is to reject evil; I reject pride and arrogance, evil conduct and a false mouth." (Cf. Prov. 15.25; 16.18, 19.) For the superscription to the third collection of Solomonic proverbs, Prov. 25.1—"The following (i.e., at least chs. 25-27, probably chs. 25-29) are also Solomonic proverbs, which were imported?/copied? by the men of King Hebekiah of Judah"—can imply that the first two Solomonic collections (see Prov. 1.1; 10.1) are known to have been edited by the men of Hezekiah and that this one is too; in that case the comma before *which* in our translation of Prov. 25.1 would be unjustified. But taking the relative pronoun as non-restrictive would be linguistically unexceptionable; and the assumption that the two preceding Solomonic collections were known to have been edited by the men of Hezekiah is, in the absence of a statement to that effect either in 1.1. or in 10.1, improbable; accordingly the punctuation of our rendering of 25.1, with a comma before *which*, is the preferable one. However, Isaiah can have known the passages cited from the first two collections even if the final redaction of these collections took place likewise only in the reign of Hezekiah.

Even clearer is the indebtedness to the Book of Proverbs of the visions of the ideal king of the future in Isa. 9.1-6 [2-7]; 11.1-5; 16.5-7. The Jerusalem doctrine of the perpetuity of the Davidic dynasty and Isaiah's adherence to it have already been discussed. But side by side with it there existed a much more ancient and much more widespread ideal of the individual king: all over western Asia we find kings represented as, or claiming to be, dispensers of justice and friends of the poor and humble. The classic Israelite crystallization of this ideal is represented by Prov. 16.21b; 20.28; 25.5b; 29.14. The affinity betwen the phraseology of these passages and that of the cited passages in Isaiah is obvious. It would therefore seem that for the social ills which he denounces, as we have seen, in diction reminiscent of Amos, Isaiah sought a remedy in a combination of the Jerusalem dynastic doctrine with the Proverbs version of the West Asiatic ideal of kingship into a vision of a charismatically endowed, just Davidic ruler of the—in his conception, of course, early—future. (The element of charisma—Heb. *ruaḥ*, literally, "spirit"—is most obvious in 11.1 ff.) A strong argument for the genuinely Isaian character of these passages is the third one. The fugitive Moabites, who have reached the extreme south of their former homeland (cf., e.g, Zoar, in 15.5), are advised in 16.1-4 to cross over into Moab's southern neighbor, Edom (if they have not already done so) and from there to dispatch an embassy to Zion to beg for asylum. Vv. 5-7, which explain why Zion is an ideal place to seek asylum in—it will henceforth be safe from marauders and ruled by an ideally just scion of David—ought properly to be followed, as indicated in the translation in a note at 16.5, by 14.32, 30a; the said envoys will be harshly rebuffed by the said prince—on the utterly Isaian ground (16.6) that Moab is notorious for monstrous arrogance and resulting wickedness! (14.30a implies that non-Israelite poor—and hence humble—folk might be considered.)

SUMMARY OF CONTENTS OF ISAIAH A

As has already been intimated, the spiritual legacy of Isaiah son of Amoz is stored in "Isaiah A," which comprises a Body, chs. 1-33, and a Historical Appendix, chs.

36-39. But that does not mean that all of these chapters were authored by him. Thus the entire Historical Appendix is merely an account, not written by Isaiah and not free from legendary traits, of incidents in which Isaiah played a part; and so are two sections in the Body: (a) 7.1-17 plus 8.8b-10 (how these pieces fit together is shown in the translation), and (b) ch. 20.

In addition, the Body contains blocks of matter of which Isaiah is neither the author nor the subject. In a publication like the present one it is not necessary to discuss or even point out every probable or possible example. But in the hope of persuading the reader that our verdicts in such matters are not arbitrary, and that where such opinions are expressed in this volume it can be assumed that at least a case can be made out for them, we shall describe here three of the larger sections whose Isaian authorship we question; and even here we shall not cite every strong argument that could be cited, but only such as are not too complicated for a layman to follow. Even so, we shall present these paragraphs in small type, and whoever wishes to may skip them on the first reading (but later reread the introduction in full!).

1. *Ch. 13:* This chapter predicts the fall of the Chaldean, or Neo-Babylonian, Kingdom, which only came into existence in the year 626 B.C.E., at least half a century after Isaiah's death. For we do not otherwise find Babylonia called Chaldea (as in our chapter v. 19) except in the Books of Jeremiah and Ezekiel (i.e., while the Chaldean Kingdom was in existence) and in Deutero-Isaiah (Isa. 43.16; 47.1, 5; 48.14, 20, i.e., immediately after the fall of the Chaldean Kingdom). [It now seems that Ur of the Chaldeans, Gen. 11.28, 31; 15.7, was situated in northern Mesopotamia and was named for a people distinct from the Chaldeans of the south.] Like others who predicted the fall of the Chaldean Kingdom (Isa. 21.1 ff., Jer. 51), the author of our chapter expected it to be effected by the Medes (v. 17); for until 550 B.C.E., only eleven years before the fall of Babylon, the Medes controlled the Median Kingdom, the only neighbor of the Chaldean Kingdom that rivaled or surpassed it in extent and power. In 550, however, Astyages, the last king of Media, was overthrown by his vassal and grandson (through his daughter) Cyrus the Persian, who took over all his dominions and conquered many more, including those of Nabonidus, the last monarch of the Neo-Babylonian Kingdom (539). To the longed-for fall of Babylon, however, our author believed that a drastic purge of the entire world—except Judah, which

had already suffered so much devastation and depopulation at the hands of the Chaldeans—was a pre-condition. Prophesying between 626 and 550, he was familiar with the prophesies of Zephaniah (ca. 630), and their influence on him is unmistakable. The expression "proudly exultant ones" (v. 3; cf. Zeph. 3.11) is a minor item, but it is nevertheless significant. Zeph. 3.11-13 echoes Isa. 3.5 ff.; 5.15-17; 14.32, 30a, etc. (just as, e.g., Zeph. 1.16 echoes Isa. 2.12, 15) and in the true spirit of Isaiah employs "proudly exulting ones" as a term of opprobrium; but Isa. 13.3 borrows it in order to use it as compliment (shades of Isaiah!). In our man's vision, not only the pride of the Chaldeans and their ilk must go by the board (vv. 11b, 19). For his fancy was caught by the slaughter and the darkness that distinguish Zephaniah's day of the Lord from Isaiah's. That he has borrowed the slaughter from Zephaniah can be seen from the footnote to our translation of Isa. 13.3: if not for Zeph. 1.7, which our author obviously had in mind, we should not know why the latter calls the Lord's henchmen His "purified (guests)." So, too, the darkness which Zephaniah is content to attribute to thick clouds ('araphel), Zeph 1.15, our man turns into a failure of the heavenly bodies themselves, Isa. 13.1, [and indeed he makes the heavens quake as well as the earth (v. 13). Whereas Zephaniah makes it clear that he is really talking only about Judah and Jerusalem (Zeph. 1.4, 10-12, 18), and that the cosmic touch (Zeph. 1.2-3) is a conventional hyperbole (as in Hos. 4.3), our man takes it literally and makes "the day of the Lord" a day of judgment upon the whole world (Isa. 13.5, 10-13)—except Judah, apparently. The result is the diametrical opposite of Isaiah's message. According to the latter, substantial depopulation (though not the unauthorized Assyrian abomination of "transpopulation") has been decreed by the Lord for Judah (6.11-12; 7.20-25) and drastic depopulation for Israel (9.13 ff.; 17.4-6, 9), while Aram is briefly threatened with a fate like Israel's (17.3); but turning the world at large into a waste is precisely the unforgivable sin of Assyria (10.7; 14.17, 20-21.)]

We have seen that the author of ch. 13 arrived at a world judgment by literalizing Zeph. 1.2-3, but from him in turn it was borrowed by several other supplementers of Isaiah A; for wherever it occurs in Isaiah A it is secondary. And one supplementer has borrowed from ch. 13 the idea of a disaster to the heavenly bodies (our v. 10) as well; in fact, he has gone further, and has made the darkening of these bodies not part of the punishment of the men on earth but a punishment of the luminaries themselves. See next paragraph.

2. *Ch. 24:* The author is obsessed with the idea of a catastrophic judgment on a human race whose corruption is comparable to that of the generation of the Flood (v. 5 is reminiscent of Gen. 6.11-12). Not only once, nor twice, but thrice, he notes that the sky will suffer the same desolation, the same seismic convulsions, and finally the same humiliation of its coryphaei as the earth: 24.4 (see footnote to the translation), v. 18 last two lines, and vv. 21-23. The last passage is the most remarkable of all: Does it mean that the heavenly bodies—or at least the two royal ones, the moon and the sun—will, like the kings of the earth, be incarcerated for a period? At any rate, these two luminaries will be put to shame—i.e., presumably their brightness will seem insignificant—when the Lord of Hosts takes up His residence in Zion and His presence is visible to His elders (v. 23). This last is a reflex of Exod. 24.9-15a, 17, and such erudite use of the Pentateuch is characteristic of very late supplementers of Isaiah A, as will be seen in the following paragraph. So it is not surprising that for "moon" and "sun" the author says *levanah* and *ḥammah*. In postbiblical Hebrew these terms have almost entirely superseded the older *yareaḥ* and *shemesh* respectively, but in the Bible the only other occurrences of them are in Song of Songs (6.10), which can safely be asserted to be one of the latest books in the Bible (perhaps as late as the second century B.C.E.) and in Isa. 30.26 in a section, Isa. 30.19-26, which cannot date much, if at all, before 400 B.C.E., as will likewise be shown in the next paragraph. For our author, however, as for that of ch. 13 which served him as model, the punishing of the world at large is only a preliminary to the punishing of the oppressive world power of his day. So ch. 24 must be regarded as continued in 25.1—26.6. 25.1-5 is a song of thanksgiving for the triumph with which ch. 24 ends. Then 25.6-8, 10-12 (25.9 interrupts the continuity and seems to belong after 26.6) go on to announce, by means of a paraphrase of Isa. 14.24-27, the world-liberating end of Assyria (see the note to the translation of 25.10). But to our author, as to the fourth century narrator in Ezra 6.22, "Assyria" means (contrary to the present writer's former view, *Encyclopaedia Judaica* IX, cls. 58-59) Mesopotamia and Iran. The rest of "The Isaiah Apocalypse"—26.7—27.13—is hard to follow at first, but 26.21 clearly again announces the coming world judgment and 27.6 ff. clearly again speaks of the Jewish restoration. ("Assyria" in 27.13 doubtless again means Mesopotamia and Iran.)

3. *30.18-26:* This is first of all an appendix, mainly in a rather pedestrian prose, to a pronouncement in Isaiah's typical lofty rhetoric. 4.3-6 and 10.24-26 are similar, if shorter

pieces, and they too are suspicious in other respects. The suspicious features of our piece are, thanks to its length, legion. Take the first verse, 30.18: it asserts that "the LORD is waiting to show you grace" and "to pardon you" because He is "a God of justice." That is rather shaky logic. Justice is giving a person what he has a legal claim to, or at least deserves as a matter of fairness or equity. Graciousness and clemency are a matter not of justice but of—well, graciousness and clemency. The paradox in our verse is a product of literary evolution. The germ of it is Jer. 31.15-17[14.16] (date ca. 620-590 B.C.E.): Rachel has for more than a century been weeping disconsolately over the exile of the tribes of Ephraim and Manasseh, which are descended from her, but now the Lord comforts her with the words: ". . . there is a *reward* to be *paid* you . . . ; they shall return from the enemy's land" (v. 16[15]). In 539 B.C.E. or shortly after, Deutero-Isaiah adapted Jeremiah's imagery in the manner which we read in this volume at Isa. 40.2, 9-11: Jerusalem's half-century of desolation has been a *period of service* by which she has made *double* atonement for her sins; she and the towns of Judah have not only worked off their debt to the Lord but have earned a credit with Him, and He is bringing their children back to them in payment. Next, the original limitation of this "reward" (or "wage," or "recompense") to the return of the exiles is lost sight of, and it is inflated to something like the role of a master race, in 61.5-8 (one must hope that the prophet intended the helots to be drawn only from among the peoples that had made exiles of the Jews, cf. 49.26; 59.22-23; 60.14); and here, for the first time, the *recompense* is motivated by the Lord's character as one who "loves *justice*." Last of all comes our verse, Isa. 30.18, whose "For the LORD is a God of justice" echoes the clause "For I the LORD love justice" of its immediate predecessor 61.5-8; but whereas the latter characterizes as justice the paying of earned wages, which makes sense, our verse confuses justice with graciousness and compassion. (The Rabbis make *din* "judgment or justice" and *raḥamim* "compassion" two distinct attributes of God, so much so that they visualize Him as occupying a different throne when He exercises the former from the one that He sits on when He exercises the latter.) Next consider Isa. 30.21-24. On close examination, these verses turn out to be an anthology of paraphrases of passages from Deuteronomy. Thus v. 21 (or, if one likes, vv. 20b-21) paraphrases as a prediction for the coming period of grace the repeated warning of Deuteronomy to the Israelites "not to turn aside to the right or to the left" from the path that it prescribes, Deut. 17.11, 20; 28.14. Similarly, Isa. 30.22 is an assurance that the community

of the future will feel toward its own idols as Deut. 7.25-26 says that the Israelites must feel toward the idols of the indigenous population of the land when they conquer it, namely, that even the gold and silver overlays of the idols must rouse in them loathing instead of cupidity. With the help of these hints, a Jewish reader who knows his prayers ought to be able to say which passage in Deuteronomy the promise of reward for good behavior in Isa. 30.23-24 expansively paraphrases. Anyway, it is Deut. 11.14-15, which promises the rain needed for growing food for man and his livestock. But our passage pedantically adds that the food that the earth will produce for man will be rich and fat, and even more pedantically distinguishes the food of livestock employed in tilling the soil and that of other livestock (i.e., sheep and goats): for the latter, abundant pasture; for the former, choice fodder. We can even explain why in v. 22 our man, instead of adopting from Deut. 7.26b the phrase "reject . . . as abominable and abhorrent," substituted for it "treat as unclean." It was because he was also thinking of Lev. 15.31, "You shall put the Israelites on guard (*wehizzartem*) against their uncleanness (*miṭṭum'atham*), lest they die through their uncleanness (*beṭum'atham*) by defiling (*beṭamme'am*) My Tabernacle, etc." That he was thinking of this verse is confirmed by the fact that he also borrowed the rare word *wehizzartem* that stands at the head of it; for in the continuation of Isa. 30.22 the received vocalization of *tizrem* is to be corrected to *tazzirem*, and the translation to "you will keep them distant like a menstruous woman," this last expression being borrowed from two verses further down in the same Leviticus passage, namely, from Lev. 15.33. Now, not only in the eighth century B.C.E. but even in the seventh and sixth there are grave reasons for doubting that a non-priest like Isaiah could have known the priestly ritual parts of the Pentateuch. Originally, priestly ritual law was studied only by priests. In *Ancient Near Eastern Texts Relating to the Old Testament* edited by J. B. Pritchard, p. 331a, ll.7-4 from bottom (so in all editions) there is a colophon to an Akkadian ritual text which designates it as "secrets" which are to be shown only to certain priests. In Judaism, the complete Torah, including the ritual laws, was eventually published, but only in the Persian Period (cf. Neh. 8). That is why throughout biblical literature only priests are recognized as authorities on ritual law, Lev. 10.8, 10-11; Deut. 24.8; Jer. 18.18; Haggai 2.10-13; Mal. 2.7-9. By our author's time, however, it could at least also be read by others; so it is no wonder that he also knew the Books of Kings, as witness v. 20a, an echo of I Ki. 22.27b. Like ch. 24, our paragraph ends (v. 26) with the two telltale neologisms kingdom. 9.7[8] ff., from 733 B.C.E., and belonging logically before 7.1–9.6[7], but reserved for present position so as to have the consecutively dated blocks 6.1 ff., 7.1 ff., and 8.1 ff. together. It gives eloquent expression to Isaiah's bitterness over Israel's attempt to oust the Davidids from Judah.

Field B, chs. 10-12, mostly from 716-715. *10.1-4a*, which is a denunciation of judicial oppression in the style of ch. 5, might date from any period in Isaiah's ministry. *10.5-15*, however, is dated by the reference to the Assyrian annexation of Carchemish in 717 (v. 9) to within a year or two after that event. Since the 730s, Isaiah has become embittered against Assyria, having noted that it was not content to plunder such nations as the Lord appointed it to plunder (8; 10.5-6) but attacked nations indiscriminately and for the purpose not of just despoiling them but of annihilating them, i.e., as 10.13 explicates, of destroying their identities by expatriation. One is tempted to surmise that the cruelty of this practice was brought home to him by the way it affected his own kindred in the erstwhile kingdom of Israel. According to the annals of King Sargon of Assyria, he carried off 27,290 inhabitants of the city of Samaria—really a substantial proportion of the population of the entire province—and settled in Samaria peoples from other regions conquered by him, in particular from North Arabia (*Ancient Near Eastern Texts Relating to the Old Testament*, pp. 284b-285a, 286a), and Isa. 10.5-15, as explained above, certainly postdates the fall of Carchemish in 717 and, hence, the exiling from Samaria of 27,290 inhabitants in 720 and very likely also the convoying of Arabians to Samaria in 715. But Isaiah feels all the more, not less, strongly the inhumanity of Sargon in treating thus the non-Israelite Carchemishites. Indeed, his thesis is that the Assyrian had no right even to plunder Carchemish, since his assignment was to do that only to (v. 6) "an ungodly nation . . . a people that provokes me"; and 8.4-8 names Damascus, Samaria, and Judah, while the term "ungodly" is applied just to Israel in 9.16 and the very word that is rendered in 10.6 "that provokes Me" is used in connection with Israel in 9.18 (there translated "anger"). Of course, Isaiah would not be Isaiah if he did not stress that this wickedness of Assyria is due to pride (vv. 12-15)! It is very likely at this point that Isaiah uttered the prediction that Assyria would be crushed in the Holy Land but for the purpose of liberating all the nations (Judah is not specially mentioned), 14.24-27. He expected this to happen very soon; for in 10.27b ff. he envisions the Assyrian advancing on Jerusalem (no doubt, in order to fulfill the old prediction that he would gravely imperil Judah though he would not succeed in conquering it, 8.7-8a), and to judge by the contemplated route (see in the translation footnote m-m on 10.27b-29) Isaiah expects Sargon to undertake this invasion of Judah on his way back from his successful North Arabian campaign in the year 715 B.C.E. In 10.33-34 the resulting decimation of Judah and Jerusalem is described, like that of Israel in 9.17, in the imagery of the destruction of forest and scrub, with the difference that in 10.33-34 the destruction takes the form of cutting, not burning; and the stumps of cut trees, says 11.1 ff., can regenerate (cf. 6.13). The stump that is left of the House of David will produce a scion who will be a charismatically wise and charismatically good king, and eventually the Holy Land will be so completely filled with goodness that there will be no room for wickedness (11.9).

II. *The Archive*, chs. 13-33, falls into three main sections: (a) The Book of Pronouncements, ch. 13-23, (b) "The Isaiah Apocalypse," chs. 24-27, (c) The Book of "Ahs," chs. 28-33.

(a) *The Book of Pronouncements, chs. 13-23*, is arranged not chronologically but geographically, in two cycles (chs. 13-20; 20-23). They both begin with Babylon and proceed to the west, the first after shifting northward to Assyria (14.24-27), the second directly (at 21.11).

Chs. 13-20. It was explained above that ch. 13 is not by Isaiah but by a seer who wrote between approximately 600 and 550 B.C.E. Of even later date, since it echoes (in slightly modified form) phrases from Zech. 2.12-16; 1.17b (520-519 B.C.E.), is the framework to the next piece. This framework (consisting of an introduction 14.1-4a and conclusion 14.22-23) represents the poem 14.4b-21 as a taunt song which the Jews *will* recite over the king of *Babylon;* but vv. 2-3, 22-23 betray such a misunderstanding of the spirit of 4b-21 that there is no reason for accepting uncritically this understanding of its purpose. An open-minded reading of the poem conveys the irresistible impression that its author is expressing his own feelings about something that *has* just *hap-*

pened in his own time; and since it is thoroughly Isaian both in diction and in spirit, what happened in Isaiah's time that could have occasioned this ode? The answer is: the death of King Sargon II of Assyria in battle and defeat in the summer of the year 705 B.C.E. It was pointed out in the section on I, Panel 3, Field B, that the most logical continuation of 10.5-15, which primarily pleads the cause of the nations at large (it does admit the right of Assyria to inflict a measure of punishment on Israel [and more mildly, on Judah] as well as on Aram, but it denies that it had a right to do even that to other nations), is 14.24-27, which predicts the shattering of Assyria for the purpose of *liberating all the nations;* Judah is of course included but not specially named. In Sargon's defeat and death in the summer of 705, Isaiah saw the fulfillment of his prediction even though he had specified (14.25) "To break Assyria in My land,/To crush him on My mountain," whereas the event of the summer of 705 took place hundreds of miles to the northeast of Israel. For the prophets were not profoundly disturbed if their prophecies were not fulfilled in detail. As a matter of fact, the event of the year 705 did not fulfill Isaiah's prediction even in substance; for the Assyrian kingdom lasted nearly a century longer, and it even held on to Judah until about a quarter of a century before the end. That will bother only those who believe in a kind of inspiration that eliminates the human personality and human fallibility. To others, this beautiful ode with its constant dwelling on the wrongs committed against "peoples," "nations," "the earth," "realms," "towns," and "the world" and its refraining from any mention of "Zion," "Jerusalem," "Judah," or "Israel" in particular (though of course Isaiah was not, in any reverse nationalism, less concerned about these than about the rest of the world!) is, like 2.2-4, one of the abiding glories of the Book of Isaiah. Because Isaiah's prophecy was not fulfilled, and because the fall of Assyria when it did come did not mean the permanent liberation even of Judah, which shortly thereafter became subject to the Chaldeans, who eventually destroyed it and carried off to Babylonia at least a third of those of its inhabitants who did not flee to Egypt and elsewhere, the editor could not imagine that the tyrant over whose fall vv. 4b.21 exult was an Assyrian king but assumed that it was the last king of Babylon that Isaiah had in mind. Now,

Cyrus, so far from destroying Babylon, did everything he could, short of withdrawing from it, to make Persian rule palatable to its people. Accordingly, our vv. 22-23 may have been inspired by the action of King Xerxes (486-465) in punishing a rebellion of Babylon by demolishing its fortifications and destroying the temple of Marduk; for as was pointed out above, the framework postdates at least the earlier years of Xerxes' predecessor Darius I.

Chs. 15-16. If 16.4b-5; 14.32, 30a; 16.6 were wanting, they would not be missed. It was explained before that just these verses are eminently in the spirit of Isaiah. The body of the "Moab" Pronouncement, however, antedates their insertion. The most plausible dating for it seems to be the time of the reconquest of Israelite Transjordan by King Jeroboam son of Joash (Jeroboam II), on which see II Ki. 14.23-25. At the time when the Israelites first occupied northern Transjordan, Moab was confined to the territory south of the wadi Arnon, having been driven from the territory between Heshbon and the Arnon by the Amorite king Sihon, whose land the Israelites conquered, Nu. 21.23-26. But we know from the inscription of King Mesha of Moab that (after the death of Ahab of Israel, II Ki. 3.5) he succeeded in wresting from Israel the land north of the Arnon at least as far as Bezer, near Heshbon; and no doubt his successors advanced still further when the Arameans forced Israel out of Transjordan altogether in the reigns of Jehu and Jehoahaz (II Ki. 10.32 ff.; 13.1-3,7). What Israel lost west of the Jordan was recovered by Joash (II Ki. 13.35), but only the latter's son Jeroboam (II) recovered the land "from Lebo of Hamath to the Sea of the Arabah (i.e., the Dead Sea)," evidently hurling back the Moabites in the process (ca. 760-750 B.C.E.). 16.13-14 seems to be even later than Isaiah's addition.

17.1-11. The coming desolation of Aram and especially of Israel, and, in the case of the latter, the reason for it.

17.12-14, 18.17. Two ahs, which ought to have been grouped with chs. 28-31; 33, perhaps after 33.

19.1-15. Obviously Isaian, though Isaiah does not give a moral ground for Egypt's imminent misfortunes—perhaps the ground is Israel's reliance upon Egypt, as in chs. 30-31. The passage 19.16 ff. is a puzzle. On the one hand, the style is not reassuring (e.g., five times "in that day"). On the other hand, v. 19 *could* be inspired by Tiglath-pileser's installing images of his gods and of himself in the royal palace of Gaza, which is near the border of Egypt, and/or by his building a palace in some locality farther south for an Arab chieftain Ibidi'lu to occupy as "Governor, or Warden of the Marches of, Misru"; while vv. 24-25 *could* have been inspired by Sargon's forcible opening of an Egyptian "sealed port" and intensifying of trade on the road which runs from the Egyptian border northward along the Philistian coast. And whatever its age or its author, this last passage, with the Lord blessing Egypt as "My people Egypt" and with Israel only one of three proverbially blessed peoples (the third being Assyria), is still another of the enduring glories of the Book of Isaiah.

Ch. 20. The year of the Assyrian capture of Ashdod is 712 B.C.E. This third person account of the part played by Isaiah in that connection seems to imply ·(1) that (v. 2) Isaiah's normal garb was a loin sackcloth (i.e., probably goat hair cloth) and sandals, and (2) that (v. 3) for three years he dispensed with even that much clothing. What actually happened is hard to say; see *Enc. Jud.* article, "Isaiah" for a suggestion. Judah was involved in the rebellion of Ashdod against Assyria, which looked to Egypt for assistance (cf. vv. 5-6). As always, Isaiah opposed an alliance with a heathen power on the (unreasonable) ground that it implied lack of faith in the Lord's ability to achieve victory unaided (see above on ch. 7).

Chs. 21-23. The whole of ch. 21 is the product of an unusual mantic personality. Vv. 1-9, anticipating the fall of Babylon into the hands of Median and Elamite besiegers, is probably, like ch. 13, from the days of the Neo-Babylonian Kingdom (or possibly from one of the periods during the Persian age when Babylon was in revolt), and the same will apply to the rest of the chapter. The verse at the end of the chapter may be, like the one at the end of the Moab pronouncement (chs. 15-16), which it resembles, an addition. Ch. 22 is Isaian, but of ch. 23 at least the prose appendix 23.15 is a postexilic addition.

(b) *"The Isaiah Apocalypse," chs. 24-27.* See above, Summary of Contents 2.

(c) The Book of "Ahs," chs. 30-33; 17.12—18.7.

III. *The Historical Appendix, chs. 36-39*

ISAIAH B, CHS. 40-66; 34-35

Generally speaking, the background of these chapters is the fall of the Chaldean Kingdom and the early years of the Persian Empire. The standard view used to be that chs. 40-48 dated from the period 547-539 B.C.E., i.e., from between the fall of Sardis, the capital of Lydia, before King Cyrus of Persia, an event which made a Persian attack on the Chaldean Kingdom seem to be the logical next step, on the one hand, and Cyrus' actual entry into Babylon, on the other, while the succeeding chapters dated from the years following the latter event, when what Cyrus did for Israel and Israel's religion fell so short of what the prophet had expected. For it was pointed out that even the last reference to Cyrus, 48.14-15, speaks only of his anticipated role in history. It should be noted, however, that Cyrus' actual measures on behalf of Israel's religion seem to be noted with satisfaction in 52.11, where see the footnote to the translation. Our interpretation of this verse jibes with the view of Haran, who has argued strongly that when the Lord asserts in 42.9 and 48.3, 6b that the "former things" that He announced have just been fulfilled and that now He is announcing "new things," the "former things" are the actual fall of Babylon to the Persians (and the "new things" the repatriation of the exiles and the rebuilding of Jerusalem and her temple). The merit of this view as against the formerly regnant one is that whereas there is no record of a Hebrew prophecy that could claim to have been fulfilled by Cyrus' capture of Sardis, there are two or three which could be pointed to with every prospect of being accepted as evidence of foreknowledge of Cyrus' conquest of Babylon. They have already been noted on pp. 13 f.; they are Isa. 13; 21.1-10; Jer. 51.11, 28. A modern reader may object that these prophecies name the Medes, not the Persians. However, when Cyrus the Persian overthrew his suzerain, Astyages, the last of the Median kings, in the year 550, he simply took over all of Astyages' dominions, and his armies and those of his successors included contingents of Median troops. It was therefore natural, at least for outsiders, to regard the kingdoms of those rulers as simply a continuation of the Median one. Thus, if a Greek writer of the Persian age wished to say "to side with the Persians" he was just as likely to say "to Medize" as "to Persize"; and when Herodotus, in his account of the campaign of Xerxes (Cyrus' third successor) in Greece, reports the message that a herald from Sparta delivered to that monarch, he makes him address the latter with the words, "O king of the Medes!" For Thucidydes, the great Persian war was *ta Mēdika* "the Median affairs." There is therefore no reason to doubt that our prophet's thesis that those earlier prophecies were vindicated by recent events was acceped by his listeners.

Our man, however, was further convinced that this event spelled the end of Israel's suffering, that the Lord would now return to Zion, bringing her children with Him; that He would reverse the miracle of the exodus from Egypt: instead of a dry path through the same He would produce a watered and shaded one straight through the Syrian Desert that lies between Babylonia and Judah (40.3-4; 41.17-19; 43.16-21; etc.). No need to bypass that desert, as, for example. Nebuchadnezzar's armies had done, by traveling up one limb of the Fertile Crescent and down the other! Why would the Lord do that? Our prophet—we will call him Deutero-Isaiah—was a successor of both Jeremiah (prophesied 626-ca. 580) and Ezekiel (prophesied 597-571). Under the influence of Jer. 31.15-17[14-16], Deutero-Isaiah says (40.1-11) that Jerusalem (and the other cities of Judah, v. 9) has, by grieving for her exiled children, earned a right to be recompensed with their return (cf. above, pp. 12-13). Under the influence of the egregious Ezekielian "consolation" (Ezek. 36.16-32), Deutero-Isaiah declares (Isa. 43.22-44.5, which read in our translation, with the notes) that Jacob is really unworthy of redemption. The present generation has neglected the sacrificial cult (as if it could help it, since the destruction of the temple!), and the people has been a sinful breed beginning with its "earliest ancestor," i.e., to judge by Hos. 12.3-5 (which becomes clearer if *Israel* is read for *Judah* in v. 3), the patriarch Jacob-Israel. That is why the Lord had to deliver this people up to taunts and jeers, even though it involved a profanation of His holy name (which was associated with Israel, so that the nations inevitably said, "That's how the people of the Lord fares: good thing we're not His people!"). And so, for His own sake, the Lord is wiping out Jacob's transgressions and will restore him to glory. See again 48.8-11. Has following both Jeremiah and Ezekiel led Deutero-Isaiah into a self-contradiction?

Of course it has, and it is no use arguing that the city could be innocent if its children were not; a city whose inhabitants are sinful is a sinful city, and if the city earned forgiveness by the suffering of loneliness, so did the people earn it by suffering the mockery that the prophet himself mentions. Moreover, see 61.7-8. The only solution is to eschew pedantry and to worry about such inconsistencies as little as the prophet himself (whose mind did not work with the precision of an electronic computer). We shall have further occasion to stress the need for flexibility.

But did the Lord have it in His power to reconstitute this scattered, disintegrating people and to reclaim and rejuvenate the land which was partly occupied by aliens and largely deserted? Did He! Why, kings were mere playthings to Him! Even the stars came out and withdrew at his command! He created them, and He knew their exact number; ditto the waters of the oceans and the earth of the continents! Were the listeners skeptical? Well, let them consider this. Only His prophets predicted the great unheavals the world had just witnessed; no other so-called god had announced them in advance to *his* people. Was that not because it was the Lord who planned those events in advance and duly brought them to pass; this meteoric rise of Cyrus, this irresistible momentum of his, that turned the weapons of kings and nations into dust and flying straw before him (41.1-4, 25-29)? This God was able to announce events beforehand, because it was He who produced them; so what events could He not produce at will? Indeed, it was Israel's duty to tell the nations that it had had foreknowledge of these events, and for that matter had had foreknowledge of many other developments throughout the ages, because its God kept it advised through His prophets. Could the nations testify the like on behalf of their gods (42.18-21; 43.6-10; 44.6-8)? If not, then only the Lord deserved to be called God. For the definition of God is: a being that can influence events favorably on behalf of His worshipers. That the Lord can influence events any way He wishes is proved by His ability to predict them; since other "gods" lack this ability, they are no gods. Here (Isa. 43.10-11) Deutero-Isaiah is again echoing a passage in Hosea (Hos. 13.1-4): When Israel incurred guilt through Baal (the reference is to Baal-peor, Hosea 9.10), its prophet (12.14), i.e., Moses, died

(13.1). And now it is sinning again, this time with idols, notably the golden calf (13.2), and again the results will be disastrous (v. 3). "But I the LORD have been your God ever since the land of Egypt; you know no God beside Me, you have no giver of triumph (*moshia'*) but Me" (v. 4). To be sure, Deutero-Isaiah does not expect the nations to come rushing to seek good fortune for themselves through this God, nor does he call upon them to do so, while Israel's own situation is rather less than favorable. But for what did the Lord give Cyrus those stunning victories if not for a purpose? Cyrus, indeed, is the Lord's shepherd (44.28)—or with a change of vocalization, "intimate"—and His chosen one (45.1). ["Chosen one" is literally "anointed one," but Isaiah B also employs the verb *mashaḥ* in 61.1 not in the sense of "to anoint" (in token of consecration to the Lord, said of men) but of "to single out" (said of the Lord); so also Ps. 105.13 calls the Patriarchs the "anointed"—again of course not literally but in the sense of "chosen ones" —and prophets of the Lord. On reflection, it will become clear that the Messiah, the king-liberator of the future, is also not actually the Anointed One but rather the Chosen One.)] The Lord, says 45.1 ff., has given those fabulous victories to Cyrus for the sake of His servant Israel and in order that all men may know from one end of the world to the other "that there is none, but Me. I the LORD both form light and create darkness, both make weal and create woe—I the LORD do all these things." (8) This recognition in turn will result in a shower of good fortune for all the earth (13). For when Cyrus builds the Lord's city and lets His exiled people go without price and without payment (14), why, even the peoples of Egypt, Nubia, and Seba—they probably seemed ultra-remote to our prophet because he lived in Babylonia—will (so goes the unbridled imagination—or perhaps, the extravagantly hyperbolic rhetoric—of our prophet) come to Israel, in self-imposed shackles, bearing their wealth as tribute, anxious to share, even as Israel's captives or vassals, in the only God who can dispense good fortune ("salvation," "vindication"). But is "salvation" obtainable by them, or must they only envy Israel? The above paraphrase of v. 8 implies the conviction that it is. Any lingering doubt should be dispersed by 45.22-25, where the interpretation implied by the translation and punctuation in the text is the only natural one. See further 49.6; 51.4, where it is surely arbitrary to interpret "light of nations/peoples" otherwise than is done in the notes to the translation, in view of 45.22-25; cf. 45.7; 59.8-10; 60.1, 20; etc. (By the way, King Azitawadd in the famous Karatepe inscriptions, boasts as follows: [Text A, col. II, II. 15-16] "For in my reign the land of the Plain of Adana enjoyed plenty and contentment; *it was never night* for the Danunians in my reign.") For from the fact (so important for him as proof that only Israel's God is real) that only Israel has (and according to 59.21 always will have) true prophets, Deutero-Isaiah infers further that Israel—no doubt mainly through the prophets in its midst, so that it does not really make much difference whether or not the word *Israel* in 49.3 is a gloss—is destined to perform for the nations what the prophets perform for Israel. For 49.1-6 is patently modeled on Jer. 1.4-10, and the outer shell of 49.6b is obviously borrowed from Jer. 1.5b-10. Of course, the inner content is completely transformed: from the mere announcing of events due to befall nations to bringing about the welfare of nations.

But is such a sentiment consistent with such arrogant ones as 49.22-23 and such vindictive ones as 49.26? Much can be said in mitigation of the former as exuberant rhetoric expressing admiration (cf. above on 45.14-17) and of the latter as applying after all only to "your oppressors"; cf. the similar expressions in 51.23; 60.14. (The latter passage, by the way, comes under the heading of exuberant rhetoric rather than of vindictiveness.) And in the case of 61.5-8, we are perhaps justified in suspecting a later hand. But above all, one must again remember that we are dealing with a blend of intellect and temperament, not with a thinking-machine. When he uttered 42.1-4; 45.22-25; 49.6; 51.4-5, he meant what these passages obviously say (not what may be wrongheadedly read into them), and they are among the glories of the Book of Isaiah.

The four sections 42.1-9; 49.1-9a; 50.4-11; 52.13-53.12 are usually spoken of as the Servant of the Lord songs. There has been much difference of opinion about these passages. A minor subject of dispute is the extent of the first three, with some critics lopping off a couple of verses at the end of each. A major question is, Who is the Servant? an individual (e.g., the, or a, prophet) or a collectivity (i.e., Israel, or part of it)? This writer prefers the collective view, but he admits that the matter is not simple. Particularly difficult is the fourth song. Here the collective interpretation is almost inevitable unless, with H. M. Orlinsky, one lops off the beginning (i.e., 52.13-15); but this procedure, which by the way is contrary to the Masorah, is adopted only for the sake of avoiding the collective interpretation; and it is arbitrary, since not only does the end of 52.15 strikingly resemble the beginning of 53 but it is the obvious introduction to the whole, corresponding to the conclusion in 53.11c-12. Only in these two passages is the speaker the Lord and are the Servant and "the many" (the masses) both spoken of in the third person. For in 53.1-6, the many speak of the Lord and the Servant in the third person; and in 53.7-11b, the prophet does the same. Now, whether 52.13-15 is included or not, the sense of the entire composition is that the Servant has suffered in order vicariously to expiate the guilt of the many. The idea of vicarious expiation is almost unparalleled (though in a sense the death of the High Priest does remove the guilt of a homicide, Nu. 35.25, and animal sacrifices do effect purgation of certain kinds of guilt, e.g., Lev. 4.26); hence a natural reluctance (shared by Kaufmann and Orlinsky, an exceptional partnership) to accept the plain meaning of the fourth Servant song. But the scientific method is to accept the unique as unique. The many could not have thought it was the Lord who had afflicted the Servant (53.4b) if it was they themselves who were maltreating him as they maltreated so many of the prophets (Orlinsky), and the "nations" and "kings" of 52.15 hardly leave any alternative to identifying the Servant with Israel (not—so Kaufmann—with the righteous in Israel, who suffered in the general national catastrophe and thus helped expiate the guilt of the guilty masses), and consequently they hardly leave any alternative to identifying the many with the Gentiles.

From ch. 56 on, one gets the distinct impression that the prophet is now living in Judah, and some of the pagan practices he scores (57.5 ff.; 65.3-5, 11; 66.3, 17) sound like confirmation that just the poorest element—economically and intellectually—had remained behind there during the Babylonian exile. Haran (and others) therefore believes that Deutero-Isaiah was among those who migrated from Babylonia to Judah. On the other hand, 64.10 probably means that not even the beginning of work on the building of a new temple, which we know from Haggai and Ezra 5 to have been made in the second year of King Darius (I), or 520 B.C.E., has yet taken place. Chs. 34-35 are either by a kindred spirit or by Deutero-Isaiah himself in his later period.

We have had occasion to refer to influences of Hosea, Jeremiah, and Ezekiel on our prophet, and there are others from Hosea and especially from Jeremiah, as also from Zephaniah, Lamentations, Psalms—and Isaiah A! (Notably, a fondness for the epithet "the Holy One of Israel.") But of course he has plenty of originality of ideas, and his style sometimes rises to heights of great lyrical beauty (e.g., ch. 40; 49.14-21; ch. 54). Isaiah B is a rich feast, and a worthy companion to Isaiah A.

H. L. GINSBERG

The Draftsmanship of Chaim Gross

Chaim Gross has long been known as one of the leading sculptors of the United States. His works can be found in a score of important American public collections. These pieces are characterized by their fascination with the human body in action, and especially with the lively world of mothers and children at play, of the circus with its acrobats, tumblers, tightrope walkers, and trapeze performers. As a carver of wood and stone, and as a modeler, he is endowed not only with skill but also with wit and humor. His creations, in several media, have offered sheer delight to all viewers.

His ability to express himself fully, using only pen and ink on paper, in a distinct, sharp, and wiry line, became known when his volume *Fantastic Drawings* was published in New York in 1956. It revealed a Gross that even those who had followed his development over the years were not aware of: capable not only of joy, but also of sadness; filled with sensuality, but also with compassion. Through his three-dimensional works he had proved himself a first-rate Realist, though one not above taking liberties with the shaping or grouping of human forms to achieve great emotional impact.

In his pen and ink drawings, he turned out to be a Surrealist of sorts, whose forms appear to have emerged rapidly from some dark pool below the threshold of consciousness—unpremeditated, spontaneous and, of course, untitled. Through them Gross was able to release painful inner sprites, to free himself of haunting memories by salvaging arbitrary images, brought forth from the world of exuberant fantasy, of myth, of memory-residue that would have perished in him and with him, still-born, had he not succeeded in embodying them for his own gratification and for the enrichment of his fellowmen.

These *Fantastic Drawings* deserve special mention here not only because they acquainted us with the "other" Gross—dark, hidden, unsuspected beneath the artist's warm and comfortable smile—but because it was their excellence that convinced the editors of The Jewish Publication Society of America that Gross was

the artist to adorn the new and scholarly translation into current English of the Book of Isaiah. The editors were aware that the customary way of "illustrating" a biblical story by means of busily and self-consciously gesticulating actors in historically "accurate" costumes and settings, with emphasis on the platitudinous and obvious, stifled rather than encouraged the reader's understanding.

The Bible calls for an artist rather than a commercial designer. In the past, we have had to make do with too many unphilosophical matter-of-fact "illustrations," especially in religious books given to the young: pictures that have no bite, that are too tidy, too timid. Limiting themselves to translating episodes from the verbal into the graphic forms, these pedestrian craftsmen failed to use their media—in a spirit akin to that of the patriarchs and sages of the past—to raise questions concerning life and death, to seek to distill the essence of the human condition, in short, to meet the challenges offered by the metaphysical nature of the text.

In Gross can be found the capacities for highlighting a deathless book to which might be applied better than to any other part of the Bible what Johann Wolfgang von Goethe wrote about the Holy Scriptures—that its sections were "complete enough to satisfy, and fragmentary enough to whet the appetite, adequately primitive to arouse, and sufficiently tender to soothe." The drawings here serve a double function: the artist is eager to communicate with his audience, yet his forms are not ends in themselves, but means to illuminate his subject matter, to shed on it a light that comes from within, not from without. Here, Gross's art is one of the soul; he permits himself to be as "grotesque" as the writer of the divine words whose mind also dwelt in the "grottoes" of darkness, from which he sent rays of consolation, of hope.

Gross is the first modern sculptor to deal with the Bible in a two-dimensional medium. I stress "modern," since the name of the greatest of all sculptors, Michelangelo Buonarroti, springs to mind as one who, in his capacity as a painter, devoted more time, effort, and of course, genius, to a pictorial rendering of the Hebrew Bible than any artist before or after him. Michelangelo, on the ceiling of the Sistine Chapel, created what has become the most celebrated ideal picture of the prophet Isaiah. He is portrayed seated on a throne, a beardless young man, looking like an athlete of ancient Greece rather than like the image of a Hebrew sage and reformer. Yet his metaphysical preoccupation is stressed by the intensity of his expression (he appears to be listening to a voice from above) and by the book he is holding, half-open, with his index finger.

Gross's Isaiah is a Semite, a richly bearded middle-aged *nabi,* but, nonetheless, more the energetic, physically impressive figure of a leader than of an anemic, bent scholar. Michelangelo's fresco has no direct bearing on the prophet's philosophy, and on the incidents involving him, whereas Gross has carefully chosen thirty-seven passages from the text, those poetic lines to which he felt a distinct spiritual response.

Michelangelo's great art is impersonal, as that of his 20th century admirer is not. Gross's pen and ink drawings, at any rate, are very subjective, very individual, very revealing, and, by the way, very unlike the preparatory sketches that he, like every one of his colleagues, makes merely to jot down his ideas quickly before approaching the block of wood, or lump of clay. For Gross does not regard drawing solely as a handmaiden to sculpture, as a first step toward three-dimensional creation, but loves it also for itself as a means to express what cannot be said with equal poignancy in other media.

To give plastic form to spiritual concepts! And to follow his hero to the no-man's-land between the conscious and the unconscious, between the visible and the invisible, between waking and dreaming that is every prophet's regular habitat. Unlike the kings, the generals, the merchants of ancient Israel, a prophet was at home in the twilight realm of ambiguity, as a seer, a poet, an artist ought to be. Poring over the manuscript of the new translation, Gross discovered, above and beyond the purely narrative, a great deal that cannot be characterized by any word but the term *surreal.* Unlike the mere illustrator, he did not shy away from the graphic rendering of fear and foreboding.

After all, he had been warned by the poets against trying to avoid the supernatural, from William Shakespeare's "There are more things on heaven and earth" to Charles Baudelaire's preference for the "monsters" of his imagination to "the triviality of positive reality." Gross is familiar with the example set by draftsmen and painters upon to prophesy doom at a time in which some of his coreligionists were experiencing unparalled peace and amazing prosperity. It was the prophet who sensed that the danger of warfare was imminent; it was the prophet who pointed out that the majority of his nation suffered heavily from exploitation by the ruling classes.

Reading the text, the artist understood only too well the scorn of the Lord—and Isaiah—for the elders and officers of Israel:

"It is you who have ravaged the vineyard;/What was robbed from the poor is in your houses./How dare you crush my people/And grind the faces of the poor?"

While some passages in the book may today be hard to grasp without an elucidating commentary, most of what it says is perfectly applicable to the 20th century. For those who believe cannot envisage God except as Isaiah's God of righteousness who loathes injustice as well as ritual divorced from ethical conduct. Those who await the Messiah cannot see him except in the image offered by our prophet: "Justice shall be the girdle of his loins, and faithfulness the girdle of his waist." Those who, like Chaim Gross, pray for a world free of violence and bloodshed are yearning for a humanity better than ours:

"They shall beat their swords into plowshares/And their spears into pruning hooks./Nation shall not take up/Sword against nation/They shall never again know war."

But these proclamations—so modern, so timeless—are only the highlights in a text filled with dramatic episodes, lyrical passages, the whimsical, the grotesque. They are merely the bones, not the flesh that can bloom, or bleed. Gross offers no abstractions as equivalents of stern dogmas. The breath of life is supplied by people, first of all the impressive omnipresent seer, and then warriors, voluptuous women, and a variety of onlookers. There are also animals—battle-trained swift horses, camels, a lion, an antelope, and a great many odd, and often frightening, birds. All over there are eloquent hands, and, alas, the inevitable lethal instruments of the warfare that was to engulf and nearly destroy Isaiah's people.

All of this serves as stage setting for the drama that each reader is required to act out, as if he were a participant in the tragic play performed in ancient Israel. By creating these pictures, the artist has become a one-man performer. He has tried to penetrate the core of meaning in the holy word, to create, who made full use of vivid fantasy to rise above the quotidian reality. William Blake cautioned, "He who does not imagine in stronger and better lineaments, and in stronger and better light than his perishing mortal eye can see, does not imagine at all." And more than a century later, the painter and printmaker Odilon Redon remarked that originality consisted of "making incredible beings live according to credible laws, in placing the logic of the possible at the service of the invisible."

Redon used the term *correspondances* to describe the relationships between the texts he read—such as tales by Edgar Allan Poe and Gustave Flaubert, and the Christian Bible's Revelation of St. John the Divine—and his lithographs inspired by them. In a similar way, Gross allowed a chapter, or even only a few lines, from Isaiah to drop into his mind and start a train of images, having a life of their own, yet always running parallel to the word that stood at the beginning. What we have on these pages, then, is essentially Gross's inner visions, those of his heart. They constitute his aesthetic homage to Isaiah, as they are fine works of art: crystal-clear design emerges victoriously from what seems to be an intricately tangled net of lines. A very personal calligraphy, seemingly unbridled and unchecked, is held together by a strong conscious control, like the many threads commanded by a puppeteer's firm hands. Gross succeeded in weaving a myriad of delicate, thin lines into tapestries in which no thread is out of order. In other words, all strokes become part of one complex, one single movement that cannot be disentangled, since all the broken lines are united into a whole, to be absorbed in its totality.

But these drawings are also moral statements by one whose talent might have failed him, had there not been a complete *correspondance* between him and the mental and spiritual giant who lived and preached and suffered at Jerusalem about twenty-seven centuries ago. To a liberal, a progressive like Gross, the tenor of Isaiah's ser-

mons was bound to be of special appeal (particularly since his eloquence created some of the world's most superb prose—or poetry). To be specific, Isaiah was called with free imagination, a piece as original, as incandescent, as the biblical passage itself. Studying and shaping the biblical episodes, the artist learned more about himself, his mortal frailties along with his higher aspirations, than he could possibly have learned from any other literature. This is hardly surprising, since nothing surpasses the Bible as an anthology of never-ending wisdom. The poet Heinrich Heine recognized the unmatched validity of the Bible. "What a book!" he exclaimed. "Great and wide as the world, rooted in the abysmal depth of creation, and rising aloft in the blue mysteries of heaven. . . . Sunrise and sunset, promise and fulfilment, birth and death, the whole human drama, everything is in this book. . . ."

He acknowledged his own intellectual debt to the Book of Books:

"It is an old simple book, modest as nature itself, and as natural; a book that appears as efficacious and unpretentious as the sun that warms, as the bread that nourishes us."

Heine, a free-thinker for a long stretch of his life, went on to say: "He who has lost his God can redesign Him in this book. He who has never known Him will inhale here the breath of God's word."

During the destruction of the Temple in Jerusalem, predicted by Isaiah, the Jews, Heine asserts, let all the precious things perish in the conflagration except for the Bible:

"This was the real treasure of the Temple."

ALFRED WERNER

The Book of Isaiah

I

¹The prophecies of Isaiah son of Amoz, who prophesied concerning Judah and Jerusalem in the reigns of Uzziah, Jotham, Ahaz, and Hezekiah, kings of Judah.

²Hear, O heavens, and give ear, O earth,
For the LORD has spoken:
"I reared children and brought them up—
And they have rebelled against Me! ·
³An ox knows its owner,
An ass its master's crib:
Israel does not know,
My people takes no thought."

⁴Ah, sinful nation!
People laden with iniquity!
Brood of evildoers!
Depraved children!
They have forsaken the LORD,
Spurned the Holy One of Israel,
Turned their backs [on Him].

⁵Why do you seek further beatings,
That you continue to offend?
Every head is ailing,
And every heart is sick.
⁶From head to foot
No spot is sound:
All bruises, and welts,

And festering sores—
Not pressed out, not bound up,
Not softened with oil.
⁷Your land is a waste,
Your cities burnt down;
Before your eyes, the yield of your soil
Is consumed by strangers—
A wasteland ᵃ⁻as overthrown by strangers!⁻ᵃ
⁸Fairᵇ Zion is left
Like a booth in a vineyard,
Like a hut in a cucumber field,
Like a city beleaguered.
⁹Had not the LORD of Hosts
Left us some survivors,
We should be like Sodom,
Another Gomorrah.

¹⁰Hear the word of the LORD,
You chieftains of Sodom;
Give ear to our God's instruction,
You folk of Gomorrah!
¹¹"What need have I of all your sacrifices?"
Says the LORD.
"I am sated with burnt offerings of rams,
And suet of fatlings,
And blood of bulls;
And I have no delight
In lambs and he-goats.
¹²That you come to appear before Me—
Who asked that of you?
ᶜ⁻Trample My courts
¹³   no more;
Bringing oblations is futile,⁻ᶜ
Incense is offensive to Me.
New moon and sabbath,
Proclaiming of solemnities,

ᵃ⁻ᵃ *Emendation yields "like Sodom overthrown"*
ᵇ   *Lit. "Daughter"*
ᶜ⁻ᶜ *Others "To trample My courts?*
     13 Bring no more vain oblations"

*d-*Assemblies with iniquity*-d*,
  I cannot abide.
¹⁴Your new moons and fixed seasons
  Fill Me with loathing;
  They are become a burden to Me,
  I cannot endure them.
¹⁵And when you lift up your hands,
  I will turn My eyes away from you;
  Though you pray at length,
  I will not listen.
  Your hands are stained with crime—
¹⁶Wash yourselves clean;
  Put your evil doings
  Away from My sight.
  Cease to do evil;
¹⁷Learn to do good.
  Devote yourselves to justice;
  *e-*Aid the wronged.*-e*
  Uphold the rights of the orphan;
  Defend the cause of the widow.

¹⁸"Come, *e-*let us reach an understanding,*-e*
  —says the LORD—
  Be your sins like crimson,
  They can turn snow-white;
  Be they red as dyed wool,
  They can become like fleece."
¹⁹If, then, you agree and give heed,
  You will eat the good things of the earth;
²⁰But if you refuse and disobey,
  *f-*You will be devoured [by] the sword.*-f*—
  For it was the LORD who spoke.

²¹Alas, she has become a harlot,
  The faithful city
  That was filled with justice,

Where righteousness dwelt—
  But now murderers.
²²Your*g* silver has turned to dross;
  *e-*Your wine is cut with water.*-e*
²³Your rulers are rogues
  And cronies of thieves,
  Every one avid for presents
  And greedy for gifts;
  They do not judge the case of the orphan,
  And the widow's cause never reaches them.

²⁴Assuredly, this is the declaration
  Of the Sovereign, the LORD of Hosts,
  The Mighty One of Israel:
  "Ah, I will get satisfaction from My foes;
  I will wreak vengeance on My enemies!
²⁵I will turn My hand against you*g*,
  And smelt out your dross *h-*as with lye,*-h*
  And remove all your slag:
²⁶I will restore your magistrates as of old,
  And your counselors as of yore.
  After that you shall be called
  City of Righteousness, Faithful City."

²⁷*i-*Zion shall be saved in the judgment;
  Her repentant ones, in the retribution.*i*
²⁸But rebels and sinners shall all be crushed,
  And those who forsake the LORD shall perish.

²⁹Truly, you*k* shall be shamed
  Because of the terebinths you desired,

d-d Septuagint "Fast and assembly"; cf. Joel 1.14
e-e Meaning of Heb uncertain
f-f Or "you will be fed the sword"
g I.e. Jerusalem
h-h Emendation yields "in a crucible"; cf. 48.10
i Others "Zion shall be saved by justice,
      Her repentant ones by righteousness"
j For this meaning cf. 5.16; 10.22
k Heb "they"

And you shall be confounded
Because of the gardens you coveted.
³⁰For you shall be like a terebinth
Wilted of leaf,
And like a garden
That has no water,
³¹¹⁻Stored wealth⁻¹ shall become as tow,
And he who amassed it a spark;
And the two shall burn together,
With none to quench.

2

¹The word that Isaiah son of Amoz prophesied concerning Judah and Jerusalem.

²In the days to come,
The Mount of the Lord's House
Shall stand firm above the mountains
And tower above the hills;
And all the nations
Shall gaze on it with joy.
³And the many peoples shall go and shall say:
"Come,
Let us go up to the Mount of the Lord,

1-1   *Connecting* ḥason *with the verb* ḥasan *("to store") in 23.18 ("treasure") in 33.6*
a   *I.e. oracles will be obtainable*
b   *More exactly, the iron points with which wooden plows were tipped*
c   *Cf. Jud. 3.2*
d   *Emendation yields "For they are full of divination
               And have abundance of soothsaying,
               Like Philistines
               And like alien folk"*
e   *Cf. Targum; lit. "children"*
f-f   *Meaning of Heb uncertain. Emendation yields "And their idols with them"; cf. vv. 17-21*

To the House of the God of Jacob;
That He may instruct us in His ways,
And that we may walk in His paths."
For instruction shall come forth^a from Zion,
The word of the Lord from Jerusalem.
⁴Thus He will judge among the nations
And arbitrate for the many peoples,
And they shall beat their swords into plowshares^b
And their spears into pruning hooks:
Nation shall not take up
Sword against nation;
They shall never again know^c war.

⁵O House of Jacob!
Come, let us walk
By the light of the Lord.
⁶For you have forsaken [the ways of] your people,
O House of Jacob!
^dFor they are full [of practices] from the East,
And of soothsaying like the Philistines;
They abound in customs^e of the aliens.
⁷Their land is full of silver and gold,
There is no limit to their treasures;
Their land is full of horses,
There is no limit to their chariots.
⁸And their land is full of idols;
They bow down to the work of their hands,
To what their own fingers have wrought.
⁹But man shall be humbled,
And mortal brought low—
^{f-}Oh, do not forgive them!^{-f}

¹⁰Go deep into the rock,
Bury yourselves in the ground,
Before the terror of the Lord
And His dread majesty!

11Man's haughty look shall be brought low,
  And the pride of mortals shall be humbled.
  None but the LORD shall be
  Exalted in that day.

12For the LORD of Hosts has ready a day
  Against all that is proud and arrogant,
  Against all that is lofty—so that it is brought low:
13Against all the cedars of Lebanon,
  Tall and stately,
  And all the oaks of Bashan;
14Against all the high mountains
  And all the lofty hills;
15Against every soaring tower
  And every mighty wall;
16Against all the ships of Tarshish
  And all the gallant barks.
17Then man's haughtiness shall be humbled
  And the pride of man brought low.
  None but the LORD shall be
  Exalted in that day.

18As for idols, they shall vanish completely.
19And men shall enter caverns in the rock
  And hollows in the ground—
  Before the terror of the LORD
  And His dread majesty,
  When He comes forth to overawe the earth.

20On that day, man shall fling away,
  To the g-flying foxes-g and the bats,
  The idols of silver
  And the idols of gold,
  Which he made for worshiping,
21And they shall enter the clefts in the rocks
  And the crevices in the cliffs,

Before the terror of the LORD
And His dread majesty,
When He comes forth to overawe the earth.

22Oh, cease to glorify man,
  Who has only a breath in his nostrils!
  For by what does he merit esteem?

3

1For lo!
  The Sovereign LORD of Hosts
  Will remove from Jerusalem and from Judah
  Prop and stay,
  Every prop of food
  And every prop of water:[a]
2Soldier and warrior,
  Magistrate and prophet,
  Augur and elder;
3Captain of fifty,
  Magnate and counselor,
  Skilled artisan and expert enchanter;[b]
4And He[c] will make boys their rulers,
  And babes shall govern them.
5So the people shall oppress one another—
  Each oppressing his fellow:
  The young shall bully the old;
  And the despised, the honored.

6For should a man seize his brother,

g-g *Exact meaning of Heb uncertain*

a *Emendation yields "clothing"; cf. v. 7; 4.1*
b *Emendation yields craftsman*
c *Heb "I"*

d·In whose father's house there is clothing:·*d*
"Come, be a chief over us,
And let this ruin*e* be under your care,"
[7]The other will thereupon swear,
"I will not be a dresser of wounds,
With no food or clothing in my own house.
You shall not make me chief of a people!"

[8]Ah, Jerusalem has stumbled,
And Judah has fallen,
Because by word and deed they insult the LORD,
Defying His majestic glance.
[9]Their partiality in judgment*f* accuses them;
They avow their sins like Sodom,
They do not conceal them.
Woe to them! For ill
Have they served themselves.
[10](Hail*g* the just man, for he shall fare well;
For he shall eat the fruit of his works.
[11]Woe to the wicked man, for he shall fare ill;
For as his hands have dealt so shall it be done to
    him.)
[12]My people's rulers are babes,
It is governed by women.*h*
O my people!
Your leaders are misleaders;
They have confused the course of your paths.

[13]The LORD stands up to plead a cause,

He rises to champion peoples.*i*
[14]The LORD will bring this charge
Against the elders and officers of His people:
"It is you who have ravaged the vineyard;
That which was robbed from the poor is in your
    houses.
[15]How dare you crush My people
And grind the faces of the poor?"—
Declares my Lord GOD of Hosts.

[16]The LORD said:
"Because the daughters of Zion
Are so vain
And walk with *j*·heads thrown back,·*j*
With eyes roving,
And with mincing gait,
Making a tinkling with their feet"—
[17]My Lord will bare*k* the pates
Of the daughters of Zion,
The LORD will uncover their heads.

[18]   In that day, my Lord will strip off the finery*l* of the anklets, the fillets, and the crescents; [19]of the eardrops, the bracelets, and the veils; [20]the turbans, the armlets, and the sashes; of the talismans and the amulets; [21]the signet rings and the nose rings; [22]of the festive robes, the mantles, and the shawls; the purses, [23]the lace gowns, and the linen vests; and the kerchiefs and the capes.

[24]And then—
Instead of perfume, there shall be rot;
And instead of an apron, a rope;
Instead of a diadem of beaten-work,
A shorn head;
Instead of a rich robe,

---

d-d   *Emendation yields "His father's son, saying,"*
e   *Meaning of Heb uncertain. Emendation yields "wound"*
f   *So Targum; cf. Deut. 1.17*
g   *Emendation yields "Happy is"*
h   *Emendation yields "boys"; cf. v. 4 (and v. 5)*
i   *Septuagint "His people"; cf. vv. 14, 15*
j-j   *Lit. "throats bent back"*
k   *So Saadia. To bare a woman's head in public was an intolerable humiliation: cf. Mishnah Baba Kamma 8:6*
l   *Many of the articles named in vv. 18-24 cannot be identified with certainty*

³"Now, then,
Dwellers of Jerusalem
And men of Judah,
You be the judges
Between Me and My vineyard:
⁴What more could have been done for My vine-
  yard
That I failed to do in it?
Why, when I hoped it would yield grapes,
Did it yield wild grapes?

⁵"Now I am going to tell you
What I will do to My vineyard:
I will remove its hedge,
That it may be ravaged;
I will break down its wall,
That it may be trampled.
⁶And I will ᵃ⁻make it a desolation⁻ᵃ;
It shall not be pruned or hoed,
And it shall be overgrown with briers and thistles.
And I will command the clouds
To drop no rain on it."

⁷For the vineyard of the LORD of Hosts
Is the House of Israel,
And the seedlings he lovingly tended
Are the men of Judah.
ᵇAnd He hoped for justice,

But, behold, injustice;
For equity,
But behold, iniquity!

⁸Ah,
Those who extend house up to house
And join field to field,
Till there is room for none but you
To dwell in the land!
⁹In my hearing [said] the LORD of Hosts:
Surely, great houses
Shall lie forlorn,
Spacious and splendid ones
Without occupants.
.¹⁰For ten acres of vineyard
Shall yield just one *bath*,ᶜ
And a field sown with a *homer* of seed
Shall yield a mere *ephah*.

¹¹Ah,
Those who chase liquor
From early in the morning,
And till late in the evening
Are inflamed by wine!
¹²ᵈ⁻Who, at their banquets,
Have⁻ᵈ harp and lute,
Tabret, flute, and wine;
But never give a thought
To the plan of the LORD,
And take no note
Of what He is designing.
¹³Assuredly,
My people will suffer exile
For not giving heed,
Its multitude victims of hunger
And its masses parched with thirst.

ᵃ⁻ᵃ *Meaning of Heb uncertain*
ᵇ   *This sentence contains two word-plays:*
        "And He hoped for mishpat,
        And there is mispah *(exact meaning uncertain);*
        For sedaqah,
        But there is se'aqah *(lit. "outcry")*
ᶜ   *I.e. of wine. The* bath *was the liquid equivalent of the*
        ephah; *and the* homer *was ten* baths *or* ephahs *(Ezek.*
        45.11)
ᵈ⁻ᵈ *Emendation yields "whose interests are"* (mish'ehem, *from*
        sha'ah *"to turn to,"* 17.7,8; 31.1)

14Assuredly,
  Sheol has opened wide its gullet
  And parted its jaws in a measureless gape;
  And down into it shall go
  That splendor and tumult,
  That din and revelry.
15 Yea, man is bowed,
  And mortal brought low,
  Brought low is the pride of the haughty.
16 And the Lord of Hosts is exalted by judgment,
  The Holy God proved holy by retribution.
17*e*Then lambs shall graze
  *a-*As in their meadows,*-a*
  And strangers shall feed
  On the ruins of the stout.

18Ah,
  Those who haul sin with cords of falsehood
  And iniquity as with cart ropes!
19Who say,*f*
  "Let Him speed, let Him hasten His purpose,
  If we are to give thought;
  Let the plans of the Holy One of Israel
  Be quickly fulfilled,
  If we are to give heed."

20Ah,
  Those who call evil good
  And good evil;
  Who present darkness as light
  And light as darkness;
  Who present bitter as sweet
  And sweet as bitter!
21Ah, Those who are so wise—
  In their own opinion;
  So clever—

In their own judgment!

22Ah,
  Those who are so doughty—
  As drinkers of wine,
  And so valiant—
  As mixers of drink!
23Who vindicate him who is in the wrong
  In return for a bribe,
  And withhold vindication
  From him who is in the right.

24Assuredly,
  As straw is consumed by a tongue of fire
  And hay *g-*shrivels as it burns,*-g*
  Their stock shall become like rot,
  And their buds shall blow away like dust.
  For they have rejected the instruction of the
    Lord of Hosts,
  Spurned the word of the Holy One of Israel.
25That is why
  The Lord's anger was roused
  Against His people,
  Why He stretched out His arm against it
  And struck it,
  So that the mountains quaked,*h*
  And its corpses lay
  Like refuse in the streets.

e   *Meaning of verse uncertain. Emendation yields*
      "The lambs shall graze
      In the pasture of the fat [rams],
      And the kids shall feed
      On the ranges of the stout [bucks]"
    The lambs and the kids are the poor (cf. 14.30,32), and the
      rams and bucks are the rich oppressors (cf. Ezek. 34.17-
      22)
f   *By way of retort to verse 12*
g-g *Emendation yields "is burned by flame"; cf. 33.11-12; 47.14*
h   *An allusion to the destructive earthquake in the reign of*
      King Uzziah: Amos 1.1; Zech. 14.5; cf. Isa. 9.18a

Yet his anger has not turned back,
And His arm is outstretched still.

²⁶He will raise an ensign to a nation*ⁱ* afar,
  Whistle to one at the end of the earth.
  There it comes with lightning speed!
²⁷In its ranks, none is weary or stumbles,
  They never sleep or slumber;
  The belts on their waists do not come loose,
  Nor do the thongs of their sandals break.
²⁸Their arrows are sharpened,
  And all their bows are drawn.
  Their horses' hoofs are like flint,
  Their chariot wheels like the whirlwind.
²⁹They have a roar like the lion's,
  They will roar like the great beasts;
  When they growl and seize a prey,
  They carry it off and none can recover it.

30   But in that day there shall resound over him a
roaring like that of the sea*ʲ*; and then he shall look
below and, behold,
  Distressing darkness, with light;
  Darkness, *ᵃ*in its lowering clouds.*ᵃ*

6

¹In the year that King Uzziah died, I beheld my
Lord seated on a high and lofty throne; and the

skirts of His robe filled the Temple. ²Seraphs
stood in attendance on Him. Each of them had
six wings: with two he covered his face, with two
he covered his legs, and with two he would fly.

³And one would call to the other,
  "Holy, holy, holy!
  The Lᴏʀᴅ of Hosts!
  His presence fills all the earth!"
4   The doorposts*ᵃ* would shake at the sound of
the one who called, and the House kept filling
with smoke. ⁵I cried,
  "Woe is me; I am lost!
  For I am a man *ᵇ*of unclean lips*ᵇ*
  And I live among a people
  Of unclean lips;
  Yet my own eyes have beheld
  The King Lᴏʀᴅ of Hosts."
⁶Then one of the seraphs flew over to me with a
live coal, which he had taken from the altar with
a pair of tongs. ⁷He touched it to my lips and
declared,
  "Now that this has touched your lips,
  Your guilt shall depart
  And your sin be purged away."

8   Then I heard the voice of my Lord saying,
"Whom shall I send? Who will go for us?" And
I said, "Here am I; send me." ⁹And He said, "Go,
say to that people:

  'Hear, indeed, but do not understand;
  See, indeed, but do not grasp.'
¹⁰Dull that people's mind,
  Stop its ears,
  And seal its eyes—

ⁱ   *Heb "nations"*
ʲ   *I.e. the* Lᴏʀᴅ *will intervene and come to his aid. Cf.
     29.6-7; 30.27. This verse may constitute a transition be-
     tween chaps. 8 and 9*

ᵃ   *Meaning of Heb uncertain*
ᵇ⁻ᵇ *I.e. speaking impiety; cf. Isa. 9.16, and contrast "a pure lip"
     in Zeph. 3.10*

Lest, seeing with its eyes
And hearing with its ears,
It also grasp with its mind,
And repent and save[c] itself."
11I asked, "How long, my Lord?" And He replied:
"Till towns lie waste without inhabitants
And houses without people,
And the ground lies waste and desolate—
12For the Lord will banish the population—
And deserted sites are many
In the midst of the land.

13But while a tenth part yet remains in it, it shall repent. It shall be ravaged, like the terebinth and the oak of which stumps are left even when they are felled: its stump shall be a holy seed."

7

1In the reign of Ahaz, son of Jotham son of Uzziah, king of Judah, King Rezin of Aram and King Pekah son of Remaliah of Israel marched upon Jerusalem to attack it; but they were not able to attack it.
2   Now, when it was reported to the House of David that Aram had allied itself with Ephraim, their hearts and the hearts of their people trembled as trees of the forest sway before a wind. 3But the Lord said to Isaiah, "Go out with your son Shear-jashub[a] to meet Ahaz at the end of the conduit of the Upper Pool, by the road of the Fuller's Field. 4And say to him: Be firm and be calm. Do not be afraid and do not lose heart on account of those two smoking stubs of firebrands, on account of the raging of Rezin and his Arameans and the son of Remaliah.[b] 5Because the Arameans—with Ephraim and the son of Remaliah—have plotted against you, saying, 6'We will march against Judah and invade and conquer it, and we will set up as king in it the son of Tabeel,' 7thus said my Lord God:

It shall not succeed,
It shall not come to pass.
8For the chief city of Aram is Damascus,
And the chief of Damascus is Rezin;
9The chief city of Ephraim is Samaria,
And the chief of Samaria is the son of Remaliah.[c]
d-And in another sixty-five years,
Ephraim shall be shattered as a people.-d
If you will not believe, for you e-cannot be trusted-e . . . "

10   The Lord spoke further to Ahaz: 11"Ask for a sign from the Lord your God, anywhere down to Sheol or up to the sky." 12But Ahaz replied, "I will not ask, and I will not test the Lord." 13"Listen, House of David," [Isaiah] retorted, "is it not enough for you to treat men as helpless that you also treat my God as helpless[f]? 14Assuredly, my Lord will give you a sign of His

c   Lit. "heal"
a   Meaning "(only) a remnant will turn back," i.e. repent; cf. 6.13;10.21
b   To refer to a person only as "the son of—" is slighting; cf. I Sam. 20.30, 31; 22.7,9,12,13. Cf. vv. 5,6,9
c   The thought is continued by 8.8b-10; cf. II Chron. 13.8-12
d-d Brought down from v. 8 for clarity
e-e Others "surely, you shall not be established"
f   By insisting on soliciting the aid of Assyria (see II Ki.16.7 ff.; cf. below, v. 20)

own accord! Look, the young woman is with child and about to give birth to a son. Let her name him Immanuel.*g* 15(By the time he learns to reject the bad and choose the good, people will be feeding on curds and honey.) 16For before the lad knows to reject the bad and choose the good, the ground whose two kings you dread shall be abandoned. 17The Lord will cause to come upon you and your people and your ancestral house such days as never have come since Ephraim turned away from Judah—that selfsame king of Assyria!*h*

18 "In that day, the Lord will whistle to the flies at the ends of the water channels of Egypt and to the bees in the land of Assyria; 19and they shall all come and alight in the rugged wadis, and in the clefts of the rocks, and in all the thornbrakes, and in all the watering places.

20 "In that day, my Lord will cut away with the razor that is hired beyond the Euphrates—with the king of Assyria*i*—the hair of the head and *j-*the hair of the feet,*-j* and it shall clip off the beard as well. 21And in that day, each man shall save alive a heifer of the herd and two animals of the flock.

22(And he shall obtain so much milk that he shall eat curds.) Thus everyone who is left in the land shall feed on curds and honey.

23 "For in that day, every spot where there could stand a thousand vines worth a thousand shekels of silver*k* shall become a wilderness of thorn bush and thistle. 24One will have to go there with bow and arrows,*l* for the country shall be all thorn bushes and thistles. 25But the perils of thorn bush and thistle shall not spread to any of the hills that could only be tilled with a hoe;*m* and here cattle shall be let loose, and *n-*sheep and goats*-n* shall tramp about."

g   Meaning "with us is God"
h   Cf. note on v. 13
i   Who was hired by Ahaz; cf. nn. on vv. 13 and 17
j-j I.e. the pubic hair
k   I.e. all the best farm land, corresponding to the hairiest parts of the body; v. 20
l   Because of dangerous beasts
m   Marginal farm land, too rocky for the plow, corresponding to areas of the body with scant hair
n-n See note at Exod. 12.3

a-a Meaning of Heb uncertain
b   I.e. "Pillage hastens, looting speeds," indicating that two cities are to be pillaged at an early date; see v. 4
c   I.e. Isaiah's wife
d-d Brought up from v. 6 for clarity
e   The conduit—and later the tunnel—of Siloam conveyed into Jerusalem the waters of Gihon, which symbolize "the Lord of Hosts who dwells on Mount Zion" (v. 18). For the nature of the rejection see note at 7.13

8

1The Lord said to me, "Get yourself a large sheet and write on it *a-*in common script*-a* 'For Maher-shalal-hash-baz*b*'; 2and call reliable witnesses, the priest Uriah and Zechariah son of Jeberechiah, to witness for Me." 3I was intimate with the prophetess,*c* and she conceived and bore a son; and the Lord said to me, "Name him Maher-shalal-hash-baz.*b* 4For before the boy learns to call 'Father' and 'Mother,' the wealth of Damascus and the spoils of Samaria, *d-*and the delights of Rezin and of the son of Remaliah,*-d* shall be carried off before the king of Assyria."

5 Again the Lord spoke to me, thus:

6"Because that people has spurned
The gently flowing waters of Siloam*e*"—
7Assuredly, my Lord will bring up against them

The mighty, massive waters of the Euphrates,
The king of Assyria and all his multitude.
It shall rise above all its channels,
And flow over all its beds,
⁸And swirl through Judah like a flash flood
Reaching up to the neck.*f*

*g*But with us is God,
Whose wings are spread
As wide as your land is broad!
⁹Band together, O peoples—you shall be broken!
Listen to this, you remotest parts of the earth:
Gird yourselves—you shall be broken;
Gird yourselves—you shall be broken!
¹⁰Hatch a plot—it shall be foiled;
Agree on action—it shall not succeed.
For with us is God!

¹¹For this is what the LORD said to me, when He
took me by the hand*h* and charged me not to
walk in the path of that people:
¹²"You must not call conspiracy*j*
All that that people calls conspiracy,*j*
Nor revere what it reveres,
Nor hold it in awe.
¹³None but the LORD of Hosts
Shall you account holy;
Give reverence to Him alone,
Hold Him alone in awe.
¹⁴He shall be *k*-for a sanctuary,
A stone-*k* men strike against:
A rock men stumble over
For the two Houses of Israel,
And a trap and a snare for those
Who dwell in Jerusalem.
¹⁵The masses shall trip over these

And shall fall and be injured,
Shall be snared and be caught.
¹⁶Bind up the message,
Seal the instruction with My disciples."

17 So I will wait for the LORD, who is hiding His
face from the House of Jacob, and I will trust in
Him. ¹⁸Here stand I and the children the LORD
has given me, as signs and portents in Israel from
the LORD of Hosts, who dwells on Mount Zion.
19 Now, should people say to you, "Inquire of
the ghosts and familiar spirits that chirp and
moan; for a people may inquire of its divine beings*l*—of the dead on behalf of the living—²⁰for
instruction and message," surely, for one who
speaks thus there shall be no dawn. ²¹*m*-And he
shall go about in it wretched and hungry; and
when he is hungry, he shall rage and revolt against
his king and his divine beings.-*m* He may turn his
face upward ²²or he may look below, but behold,
Distress and darkness, *n*-with no daybreak-*n*;
Straitness and gloom, *n*-with no dawn.-*n*
23 For *o*-if there were to be-*o* any break of day for
that land which is in straits, only the former
[king] would have brought abasement to the land
of Zebulun and the land of Naphtali—while the

f   *I.e. Judah shall be imperiled, but, in contrast to Aram and
Ephraim (v. 4), not destroyed*
g   *See note c at 7.9*
h   *I.e. singled me out; cf. 41.10, 13; 42.6; 45.1; Jer. 31.32 [31]*
i   *The Heb forms here and in vv. 13 and 19 are plural, to
include the disciples (v. 16) and the children (v. 18)*
j   *Meaning of Heb uncertain. Emendation yields "holy"; cf.
v. 13*
k-k *Emendation yields:*
                        . . . for His holy domain (cf. Ps. 114.2)
                    A stone . . .
l   *I.e. the shades of the dead; cf. I Sam. 28.13*
m-m *This sentence would read more logically after v. 22*
n-n *Meaning of Heb uncertain*
o-o *So 1QIsa; the others have "there is not"*

later one would have brought honor to the way of the Sea, the other side of the Jordan, and Galilee of the Nations.*p*

9

¹*ᵃ*The people that walked in darkness
Have seen a brilliant light;
On those who dwelt in a land of gloom
Light has dawned.
²You have magnified that nation,
Have given it great joy;
They have rejoiced before You
As they rejoice at reaping time,
As they exult
When dividing spoil.

³For the yoke that they bore
And the stick on their back—
The rod of their taskmaster—
You have broken as on the day of Midian.*b*
⁴Truly, all the boots put on *c*to stamp with*c*
And all the garments donned in infamy
Have been fed to the flames,
Devoured by fire.

⁵For a child has been born to us,
A son has been given us.
And authority has settled on his shoulders.
He has been named
"The Mighty God is planning grace;*d*
The Eternal Father, a peaceable ruler"—
⁶In token of abundant authority
And of peace without limit
Upon David's throne and kingdom,
That it may be firmly established
In justice and in equity
Now and evermore.
The zeal of the LORD of Hosts
Shall bring this to pass.

⁷My Lord
*ᵉ*Let loose a word*ᵉ* against Jacob
And it fell upon Israel.
⁸But all the people noted—
Ephraim and the inhabitants of Samaria—
In arrogance and haughtiness:
⁹"Bricks have fallen—
We'll rebuild with dressed stone;
Sycamores have been felled—
We'll make cedars grow back!"
¹⁰So the LORD let *f*the enemies of Rezin*f*
Triumph over it
And stirred up its foes—
¹¹Aram from the east
And Philistia from the west—
Who devoured Israel
With greedy mouths.

Yet His anger has not turned back,
And His arm is outstretched still.

---

p Meaning of verse uncertain. The rendering here assumes that "the former [king]" refers to Pekah (cf. II Ki. 15.29) and "the later" to Hoshea (ibid. 30). For the construction lu . . . ka'eth, see Judg. 13.23

a See note j at 5.30
b See Judg. 7-8
c-c Meaning of Heb uncertain; emendation yields "in wickedness": cf. Targum
d As in 25.1. Pele also has this meaning in Pss. 88.11, 13; 89.6
e-e Septuagint reads "Let loose pestilence"; cf. Amos 4.10. In vv. 7-20 Isaiah alludes to and builds upon Amos 4.10-12
f-f Emendation yields "its enemies"

¹²For the people has not turned back
To Him who struck it
And has not sought
The Lord of Hosts.
¹³So the Lord will cut off from Israel
Head and tail,
Palm branch and reed,
In a single day.
¹⁴Elders *g-*and magnates*-g*—
Such are the heads;
Prophets who give false instruction—
Such are the tails*h*;
¹⁵That people's leaders have been misleaders,
So they that are led have been confused.
¹⁶That is why my Lord
Will not spare*i* their youths,
Nor show compassion
To their orphans and widows;
For all are ungodly and wicked,
And every mouth speaks impiety.
¹⁷Already wickedness has blazed forth like a fire
Devouring thorn and thistle.
It has kindled the thickets of the wood,
*j-*Which have turned into billowing smoke.*-j*

*k-*Yet His anger has not turned back,
And His arm is outstretched still.*-k*

¹⁸By the anger of the Lord of Hosts,
The earth was shaken.*l*
Next, the people became like devouring fire:
No man spared his countryman.
¹⁹They snatched on the right, but remained hungry,
And consumed on the left without being sated.
Each devoured the flesh of his *m-*own kindred*-m*—

²⁰Manasseh Ephraim's and Ephraim Manasseh's,*n*
And both of them against Judah!*o*

Yet His anger has not turned back,
And His arm is outstretched still.

IO

¹Ha!
Those who write out evil writs
And compose iniquitous documents,
²To subvert the cause of the poor,
To rob of their rights the needy of My people;
That widows may be their spoil,
And fatherless children their booty!
³What will you do on the day of punishment,
When the calamity comes from afar?
To whom will you flee for help,
And how will you save your carcasses*a*
⁴From collapsing under [fellow] prisoners,
From falling beneath the slain?

Yet His anger has not turned back,
And his arm is outstretched still.

g-g *Emendation yields "who practice partiality"*
h   *Emendation yields "palm branches," the elders and the prophets are the leaders, the people are the led; cf. 3.1-2, 12*
i   *Cf. Arabic samuḥa*
j-j *Meaning of Heb uncertain*
k-k *Moved down from v. 16 for clarity*
l   *Cf. note at 5.25*
m-m *Meaning of Heb uncertain. Emendation yields "fellow"; cf. Targum*
n   *Alludes to the civil wars of II Ki. 15.10, 14-16, 25*
o   *Cf. 7.1-9*

a   *Compare the rendering of kabod in v. 16, and in 17.4*

⁵Ha!
 Assyria, rod of My anger,
 ᵇ⁻In whose hand, as a staff, is My fury!⁻ᵇ
⁶I send him against an ungodly nation,
 I charge him against a people that provokes Me,
 To take its spoil and to seize its booty
 And to make it a thing trampled
 Like the mire of the streets.
⁷But he has evil plans,
 His mind harbors evil designs;
 For he means to destroy,
 To wipe out nations, not a few.
⁸For he thinks,
 "After all, ᶜ⁻I have kings as my captains!⁻ᶜ
⁹Was Calno any different from Carchemish?
 Or Hamath from Arpad?
 Or Samaria from Damascus?
¹⁰ᵈSince I was able to seize
 Those kingdoms of idols and their graven images,
 Whose images exceed
 Jerusalem's and Samaria's,
¹¹Shall I not do to Jerusalem and her images
 What I did to Samaria and her idols?"

12   But when my Lord has carried out all his pur-
     pose on Mount Zion and in Jerusalem, Heᵉ will
     punish the majestic pride and overbearing arro-

gance of the king of Assyria. ¹³For he thought,
 "By the might of my hand have I wrought it,
 By my skill, for I am clever:
 I have erased the borders of peoples;
 I have plundered their treasures
 And exiled their vast populations.
¹⁴I was able to seize, like a nest,
 The wealth of peoples;
 As one gathers abandoned eggs
 Did I gather all the earth:
 Nothing so much as flapped a wing
 Or opened a mouth to peep."

¹⁵Does an ax boast over him who hews with it,
 Or a saw magnify itself above him who wields it?
 As though the rod swung him who lifts it,
 As though the staff lifted the manᶠ!

¹⁶Assuredly,
 The Sovereign LORD of Hosts will send
 A wasting away in itsᵍ fatness;
 And under its bodyʰ shall burn
 A burning like that of fire,
 ⁱ⁻Destroying frame and flesh.
 It shall be like a sick man who pines away.⁻ⁱ
¹⁷Yea, the Light of Israel will be fire
 And its Holy One flame,
 Which will burn and consume its thorns
 And its thistles in a single day,
¹⁸And the mass of its scrub and its farm land.
¹⁹What trees remain of its scrub
 Shall be so few that a boy may record them.

²⁰And in that day,
 The remnant of Israel
 And the escaped of Jacob

ᵇ⁻ᵇ *Emendation yields "Who is a staff in the hand of My*
      wrath"
ᶜ⁻ᶜ *Emendation yields "all the kingdoms fared alike!"*
ᵈ   *Emendation yields*
          "Since I was able to seize
          Those kingdoms and their images,
          What is Jerusalem
          And what is Samaria?"
ᵉ   *Heb "I"*
ᶠ   *Lit. "not-wood"*
ᵍ   *Presumably Israel's. These verses fit well after 9.16*
ʰ   *Cf. the rendering of kabod in 10.3 and 17.4, and in Gen. 49.6*
ⁱ⁻ⁱ *Brought up from v. 18 for clarity*

Shall lean no more upon him that beats it,[j]
But shall lean sincerely
On the LORD, the Holy One of Israel.
²¹Only a remnant shall return,
Only a remnant of Jacob,
To Mighty God.
²²Even if your people, O Israel,
Should be as the sands of the sea,
Only a remnant of it shall return.
Destruction is decreed;
Retribution comes like a flood!
²³For my Lord GOD of Hosts is carrying out
A decree of destruction upon all the land.

²⁴ Assuredly, thus said my Lord GOD of Hosts: "O My people that dwells in Zion, have no fear of Assyria, who beats you with a rod and wields his staff over you as did the Egyptians. ²⁵For very soon My wrath will have spent itself, and [k]My anger that was bent on wasting them."[-k] ²⁶The LORD of Hosts will brandish a scourge over him as when He beat Midian at the Rock of Oreb,[l] and will wield His staff as He did over the Egyptians by the sea.

²⁷And in that day,
His burden shall drop from your back,
[m]And his yoke from your neck;
The yoke shall be destroyed because of fatness.

²⁸He advanced upon Aiath,
He proceeded to Migron,
At Michmas he deposited his baggage.
²⁹They made the crossing;
"Geba is to be our night quarters!"[-m]

Ramah was alarmed;
Gibeah of Saul took to flight.
³⁰"Give a shrill cry, O Bath-gallim!
Hearken, Laishah!
Take up the cry, Anathoth!"
³¹Madmenah ran away;
The dwellers of Gebim sought refuge.
³²This same day at Nob
He shall stand and wave his hand.[n]

O mount of Fair Zion!
O hill of Jerusalem!
³³Lo! The Sovereign LORD of Hosts
Will hew off the tree-crowns with an ax:
The tall ones shall be felled,
The lofty ones cut down:
³⁴The thickets of the forest shall be hacked away
   with iron,
And the Lebanon trees shall fall [o]in their
   majesty.[-o]

j   *I.e. upon Assyria (see v. 24). Ahaz's reliance on Assyria was interpreted by Isaiah as lack of faith in the Lord; see 7.13 with note*
k-k *Presumably Assyria; meaning of Heb uncertain. Emendation yields "My anger against the world shall cease"*
l   *See Judg. 7.25*
m-m *Emendation yields*

   "And his yoke shall leave your neck.

   He came up from Jeshimon
28   *By the ascent of Aiath,*
   He proceeded to Migron;
   At Michmas he commanded his forces;
29 *'Make the crossing;*
   Geba is to be our night quarters!'"
   Jeshimon is the southeast corner of the Jordan Valley, Nu. 21.20: 23.28; Aiath is elsewhere called Ai
n   *I.e. the Assyrian king, arriving at Nob (close to Jerusalem), shall beckon his army onward; cf. Isa. 13.2*
o-o *Or "by the bronze," connecting Heb 'addir with Akkadian urudu, "bronze"*

11

¹But a shoot shall grow out of the stump of Jesse,
  A twig shall branch off from his stock.
²The spirit of the LORD shall alight upon him:
  A spirit of wisdom and insight,
  A spirit of counsel and valor,
  A spirit of devotion and reverence for the LORD.
³ᵃ⁻He shall sense the truth⁻ᵃ by his reverence for
    the LORD:
  He shall not judge by what his eyes behold,
  Nor decide by what his ears perceive.
⁴Thus he shall judge the poor with equity
  And decide with justice for the lowly of the land.
  He shall strike down a landᵇ with the rod of his
    mouth
  And slay the wicked with the breath of his lips.
⁵Justice shall be the girdle of his loins,
  And faithfulness the girdle of his waist.
⁶The wolf shall dwell with the lamb,
  The leopard lie down with the kid;
  ᶜ⁻The calf, the beast of prey, and the fatling⁻ᶜ
    together,
  With a little boy to herd them.
⁷The cow and the bear shall graze,
  Their young shall lie down together;
  And the lion, like the ox, shall eat straw.
⁸A babe shall play
  Over a viper's hole,

And an infant passᵈ his hand
  Over an adder's den.
⁹In all of ᵉ⁻My sacred mount⁻ᵉ
  Nothing evil or vile shall be done;
  For the land shall be filled with devotion to the
    LORD
  As water covers the sea.

¹⁰In that day,
  The stock of Jesse that has remained standing
  Shall become a standard to nations—
  Peoples shall seek his counsel,
  And his abode shall be honored.

¹¹   In that day, My Lord will apply His hand
again to redeeming the other partᶠ of His people
from Assyria—as also from Egypt, Pathros, Nubia,
Elam, Shinar, Hamath, and the coastlands.

¹²He will hold up a signal to the nations
  And assemble the banished of Israel,
  And gather the dispersed of Judah
  From the four corners of the earth.

¹³Then Ephraim's envy shall cease
  And Judah's harassment shall end;
  Ephraim shall not envy Judah,
  And Judah shall not harass Ephraim.
¹⁴They shall pounce on the back of Philistia to the
    west,
  And together plunder the peoples of the east;
  Edom and Moab shall be subject to them
  And the children of Ammon shall obey them.

¹⁵   The LORD will dry up the tongue of the Egyptian sea.—He will raise His hand over the Eu-

a-a   Lit. "His sensing (shall be)"; meaning of Heb uncertain
b   Emendation yields "the ruthless"
c-c   1QIsᵃ reads: "The calf and the beast of prey shall feed"; so
        too the Septuagint
d   Meaning of Heb uncertain
e-e   I.e. the Holy Land; cf. Exod. 15.17; Ps. 78.54
f   I.e. the part outside the Holy Land; lit. "the rest that will
        remain"

phrates with the might*d* of His wind and break it into seven wadis, so that it can be trodden dry-shod. ¹⁶Thus there shall be a highway for the other part*f* of His people out of Assyria, such as there was for Israel when it left the land of Egypt.

I2

¹In that day, you shall say:
"I give thanks to You, O Lᴏʀᴅ!
Although You were wroth with me,
Your wrath has turned back and You comfort
    me,
²Behold the God who gives me triumph!
I am confident, unafraid;
For Yah the Lᴏʀᴅ is my strength and might,*a*
And He has been my deliverance."

³Joyfully shall you draw water
From the fountains of triumph,
⁴And you shall say on that day:
"Praise the Lᴏʀᴅ, proclaim His name.
⁵Hymn the Lᴏʀᴅ,
For He has done gloriously;
Let this be made known
In all the world!
⁶Oh, shout for joy,
You who dwell in Zion!
For great in your midst
Is the Holy One of Israel."

I3

¹The "Babylon" Pronouncement, a prophecy of Isaiah son of Amoz.

²"Raise a standard upon a bare hill,
Cry aloud to them;
Wave a hand, and let them enter
The gates of the nobles!
³I have summoned My purified guests
For My wrath;
Behold, I have called My stalwarts,
My proudly exultant ones."*a*

⁴Hark! a tumult on the mountains—
As of*b* a mighty force;
Hark! an uproar of kingdoms,
Nations assembling!
The Lᴏʀᴅ of Hosts is mustering
A host for war.
⁵They come from a distant land,
From the end of the sky—
The Lᴏʀᴅ with the weapons of His wrath—
To ravage all the earth!

⁶Howl!
For the day of the Lᴏʀᴅ is near;
It shall come like havoc from Shaddai.*c*

d   *Meaning of Heb uncertain*
f   *I.e. the part outside the Holy Land; lit. "the rest that will*
     remain"

a   *Others "song"*

a   *The impending slaughter is spoken of as a sacrificial meal,*
     for which the guests were notified to purify themselves
     ritually; cf. Zeph. 1.7
b   *Meaning of Heb uncertain*
c   *Traditionally rendered "the Almighty"*

⁷Therefore all hands shall grow limp,
  And all men's hearts shall sink;
⁸And, overcome by terror,
  They shall be seized by pangs and throes,
  Writhe like a woman in travail.
  They shall gaze at each other in horror,
  Their faces ᵈ⁻livid with fright.⁻ᵈ

⁹Lo! The day of the Lᴏʀᴅ is coming
  With pitiless fury and wrath,
  To make the earth a desolation,
  To wipe out the sinners upon it.
¹⁰The stars and constellations of heaven
  Shall not give off their light;
  The sun shall be dark when it rises,
  And the moon shall diffuse no glow.

¹¹"And I will requite to the world its evil,
  And to the wicked their iniquity;
  I will put an end to the pride of the arrogant
  And humble the haughtiness of tyrants.
¹²I will make people scarcer than fine gold,
  And men than gold of Ophir."

¹³Therefore ᵉ⁻shall heaven be shaken,⁻ᵉ
  And earth leap out of its place,
  At the fury of the Lᴏʀᴅ of Hosts
  On the day of His burning wrath.
¹⁴Then like gazelles that are chased,
  And like sheep that no man gathers,

Each man shall ᶠ⁻turn back⁻ᶠ to his people,
  They shall flee everyone to his land.
¹⁵All who remain shall be pierced through,
  All who ᵇ⁻are caught⁻ᵇ
  Shall fall by the sword.
¹⁶And their babes shall be dashed to pieces in their
    sight,
  Their homes shall be plundered,
  And their wives shall be raped.

¹⁷"Behold,
  I stir up the Medes against them,
  Who do not value silver
  Or delight in gold.
¹⁸Their bows shall shatter the young;
  They shall show no pity to infants,
  They shall not spare the children."

¹⁹And Babylon, glory of kingdoms,
  Proud splendor of the Chaldeans,
  Shall become like Sodom and Gomorrah
  Overturned by God.
²⁰Nevermore shall it be settled
  Nor dwelt in through all the ages.
  There no Arab shall pitch his tent,
  There no shepherds make flocks lie down.
²¹But beasts ᵇ shall lie down there,
  And the houses be filled with owls ᵇ;
  There shall ostriches make their home, ᵍ
  And there shall satyrs dance.
²²And jackals ᵇ shall abide ᵍ in its castles
  And dragons ᵇ in the palaces of pleasure.

Her hour is close at hand;
Her days will not be long.

ᵈ⁻ᵈ *Taking the root* lhb *as a variant of* bhl: *others "shall be*
    faces of flame"
ᵉ⁻ᵉ *Lit. "I will shake heaven"*
ᶠ⁻ᶠ *Meaning of Heb uncertain; emendation yields "flee"*
ᵍ *Meaning of Heb uncertain; cf. Deut. 33.28*

14

¹But the LORD will pardon Jacob, and will again choose Israel, and will settle them on their own soil. And strangers shall join them and shall cleave to the House of Jacob. ²For peoples shall take them*a* and bring them to their homeland; and the House of Israel shall possess them*b* as slaves and handmaids on the soil of the LORD. They shall be captors of their captors and masters to their taskmasters.

³ And when the LORD has given you rest from your sorrow and trouble, and from the hard service that you were made to serve, ⁴you shall recite this song of scorn over the king of Babylon:
How is the taskmaster vanished,
How is oppression*c* ended!
⁵The LORD has broken the staff of the wicked,
The rod of tyrants,
⁶That smote peoples in wrath
With stroke unceasing,
That belabored nations in fury
In relentless pursuit.

⁷All the earth is calm, untroubled;
Loudly it cheers.
⁸Even pines rejoice at your fate,
And cedars of Lebanon:
"Now that you have lain down,
None shall come up to fell us."

⁹Sheol below was astir
To greet your coming—
Rousing for you the shades
Of all earth's chieftains,

Raising from their thrones
All the kings of nations.
¹⁰All speak up and say to you,
"So you have been stricken as we were,
You have become like us!
¹¹Your pomp is brought down to Sheol,
And the strains of your lutes!
Worms are to be your bed,
Maggots your blanket!"

¹²How are you fallen from heaven,
O Shining One, son of Dawn!*d*
How are you felled to earth,
O vanquisher of nations!

¹³Once you thought in your heart,
"I will climb to the sky;
Higher than the stars of God
Will I set my throne.
I will sit in the mount of assembly,*e*
On the top of heaven:*f*
¹⁴I will mount the back of a cloud—
I will match the Most High."
¹⁵Instead, you are brought down to Sheol,
To *g*the bottom of the Pit.*-g*
¹⁶They who behold you stare;
They peer at you closely:
"Is this the man
Who shook the earth,
Who made realms tremble,

a   *I.e. the House of Jacob*
b   *I.e. the peoples*
c   *Reading* marhebah *with 1QIsᵃ (cf. Septuagint). The traditional reading* madhebah *is of unknown meaning*
d   *A character in some lost myth*
e   *I.e. the assembly of the gods in council*
f   *Cf. Job 26.7; others "in the uttermost parts of the north"*
g-g *A region of the netherworld reserved for those who have not received decent buri*a*l. Cf. Ezek. 32.21 ff.*

¹⁷Who made the world like a waste
  And wrecked its towns,
  ^{h-}Who never released his prisoners to their
    homes?"
¹⁸All the kings of nations
  Were laid, every one, in honor^{-h}
  Each in his tomb;
¹⁹While you were left lying unburied,
  Like loathsome carrion,ⁱ
  Like a trampled corpse
  [In] the clothing of slain gashed by the sword
  Who sink to the very stones of the Pit.
²⁰You shall not have a burial like them;
  Because you destroyed ^{j-}your country,
  Murdered your people.^{-j}

  Let the breed of evildoers
  Nevermore be named!
²¹Prepare a slaughtering block for his sons
  Because of the guilt of their father.^k
  Let them not arise to possess the earth!
  Then the world's face shall be covered with
    towns.

h-h *Emendation yields*
        "Who chained to his palace gate
        All the kings of nations?
        Yet they were all laid in honor . . ."
    The practice of chaining captive chieftains to gates is at-
    tested in Mesopotamia
i   *So several ancient versions; cf. postbiblical* neṣel, *"Putrefy-*
    ing flesh or blood"
j-j *Emendation yields*
        " . . . countries,
        Murdered peoples"
k   *Heb "fathers"*
l   *Meaning of Heb uncertain*
m   *Heb "mountains"; for the designation of the entire land of*
    Israel as the Lord's mountain, cf. 11.9
n   *Heb "his." The last two lines of this v. would read better*
    after v. 26
o   *Others "fiery serpent"; cf. Nu. 21.6, 8*
p-p *Emendation yields "It shall kill your offspring with its*
    venom"
q-q *Meaning of Heb uncertain; the rendering "stout one" is*
    suggested by the Syriac 'ashshīn

²² I will rise up against them—declares the Lord
  of Hosts—and will wipe out from Babylon name
  and remnant, kith and kin—declares the Lord—
  ²³and I will make it a home of bitterns,^l pools of
  water. I will sweep it with a broom of extermina-
  tion—declares the Lord of Hosts.

²⁴The Lord of Hosts has sworn this oath:
  "As I have designed, so shall it happen;
  What I have planned, that shall come to pass:
²⁵To break Assyria in My land,
  To crush him on My mountain."^m
  And his yoke shall drop off them,
  And his burden shall drop from theirⁿ backs.
²⁶That is the plan that is planned
  For all the earth;
  That is why an arm is poised
  Over all the nations.
²⁷For the Lord of Hosts has planned,
  Who then can foil it?
  It is His arm that is poised,
  And who can stay it?

²⁸ This pronouncement was made in the year that
  King Ahaz died:

²⁹Rejoice not, all Philistia,
  Because the staff of him that beat you is broken.
  For from the stock of a snake there sprouts an asp,
  A flying seraph^o branches out from it.
³⁰^{p-}I will kill your stock by famine,^{-p}
  And it shall slay the very last of you.
³¹Howl, O gate; cry out, O city;
  Quake, all Philistia!
  ^{q-}For a stout one is coming from the north
  And there is no straggler in his ranks.^{-q}

32And what will he answer the messengers of any
   nation?
  That Zion has been established by the LORD:
  In it, the needy of His people shall find shelter,
  ʳThe first-born of the poor shall graze,
  And the destitute lie down secure.ʳ

15

1The "Moab" Pronouncement.

  Ah, in the night Ar was sacked,
  Moab was ruined;
  Ah, in the night Kir was sacked,
  Moab was ruined.

2He went up to the temple to weep,
  Dibonᵃ [went] to the outdoor shrines.
  Over Nebo and Medeba
  Moab is wailing;
  On every head is baldness,
  Every beard is shorn.
3In its streets, they are girt with sackcloth;
  On its roofs, in its squares,
  Everyone is wailing,
  Streaming with tears.
4Heshbon and Elealeh cry out,
  Their voice carries to Jahaz.

  Therefore,
  ᵇThe shock troops of Moab shout,ᵇ
  His body is convulsed.
5My heart cries out for Moab—
  His fugitives flee down to Zoar,
  To Eglath-shelishiyah.

For the ascent of Luhith
They ascend with weeping;
On the road to Horonaim
They raise a cry of anguish.

6Ah, the waters of Nimrim
  Are become a desolation;
  The grass is sear,
  The herbage is gone,
  Vegetation is vanished.

7Therefore,
  The gains they have made, and their stores,
  They carry to the Wadi of Willows.

8Ah, the cry has compassed
  The country of Moab:
  All the way to Eglaim her wailing,
  Even at Beer-elim her wailing!

9Ah, the waters of Dimon are full of bloodᶜ
  For I pour added [water] on Dimon;
  I drenchᵈ it—for Moab's refugees—
  With soilᵉ for its remnant.

16

1ᵃDispatch as messenger
  The ruler of the land,

---

r-r *Brought down from v. 30 for clarity*

a *Regarded as the principal city of Moab*
b-b *Change of vocalization yields "The loins of Moab are
     trembling,"*
c *Emendation yields "tears"*
d *Cf. 16.9*
e *Emendation yields "tears"; cf. Ugaritic 'dm‛t*

a *Meaning of vv. 1 and 2 uncertain*

From Sela in the wilderness
To the mount of Fair Zion:

²"Like fugitive birds,
Like nestlings driven away,
Moab's villagers linger
By the fords of the Arnon.
³Give advice,
^{b-}Offer counsel.^{-b}
At high noon make
Your shadow like night:
Conceal the outcasts,
Betray not the fugitives.
^{4c-}Let Moab's outcasts^{-c}
Find asylum in you;
Be a shelter for them
Against the despoiler."

For violence has vanished,
Rapine is ended,
And marauders have perished from this land.
⁵And a throne shall be established in goodness
In the tent of David,
And on it shall sit in faithfulness
A ruler devoted to justice
And zealous for equity.^d

⁶"We have heard of Moab's pride—
Most haughty is he—
Of his pride and haughtiness and arrogance,

And of the iniquity in him."^e

⁷Ah, let Moab howl;
Let all in Moab howl for it!
For the raisin cakes^f of Kir-hareseth
You shall moan most pitifully.
⁸The vineyards of Heshbon are withered,
And the vines of Sibmah,
Whose tendrils spread
^{b-}To Baale-goiim,^{-b}
And reached to Jazer,
And strayed to the desert;
Whose shoots spread out
And crossed the sea.

⁹Therefore,
As I weep for Jazer,
So I weep for Sibmah's vines;
O Heshbon and Elealeh,
I drench you with my tears.
^{g-}Ended are the shouts
Over your fig and grain harvests.^{-g}
¹⁰Rejoicing and gladness
Are gone from the farm land;
In the vineyards no shouting
Or cheering is heard.
No more does the treader
Tread wine in the presses—
The shouts have been silenced.^h

¹¹Therefore,
Like a lyre my heart moans for Moab,
And my very soul for Kir-heres.

¹²   And when it has become apparent that Moab
has gained nothing in the outdoor shrine, he shall

come to pray in his temple—but to no avail.

13   That is the word that the Lord spoke concerning Moab long ago. ¹⁴And now the Lord has spoken: In three years, fixed like the years of a hired laborer, Moab's population, with all its huge multitude, shall shrink. Only a remnant shall be left, of no consequence.

17

¹The "Damascus" Pronouncement.

Behold,
Damascus shall cease to be a city;
It shall become a heap of ruins.
²ᵃ⁻The towns of Aroer shall be deserted;⁻ᵃ
They shall be a place for flocks
To lie down, with none disturbing.

³Fortresses shall cease from Ephraim,ᵇ
And sovereignty from Damascus;
The remnant of Aram shall become
Like the mass of Israelites—
Declares the Lord of Hosts.

⁴In that day,
The mass of Jacob shall dwindle,
And the fatness of his body become lean:
⁵After being like the standing grain
Harvested by the reaper—
Who reaps ears by the armful—
He shall be like the ears that are gleaned
In the Valley of Rephaim.

⁶Only gleanings shall be left of him,
As when one beats an olive tree:
Two berries or three on the topmost branch,
Four or five ᶜ⁻on the boughs of the crown.⁻ᶜ—
Declares the Lord, the God of Israel.

⁷   In that day, men shall turn to their Maker, their eyes look to the Holy One of Israel; ⁸they shall not turn to the altars that their own hands made, or look to the cult poles and incense stands that their own fingers wrought.

⁹   In that day, their fortress cities shall be like the deserted sites which ᵈ⁻the Horesh and the Amir⁻ᵈ abandoned because of the Israelites; and there shall be desolation.

¹⁰Truly, you have forgotten the God who saves you
And have not remembered the Rock who shelters you;
That is why, though you plant a delightfulᵉ sapling,
What you sow proves a disappointing slip.
¹¹On the day that you plant, you see it grow;
On the morning you sow, you see it bud—
But the branches wither away
On a day of sickness and mortal agony.

¹²Ah, the roar of many peoples
That roar as roars the sea,
The rage of nations that rage

a-a   *Emendation yields (cf. Septuagint) "Its towns shall be deserted for evermore"*
b   *Emendation yields "Aram"*
c-c   *Lit. "on her boughs, the many-branched one"*
d-d   *Septuagint reads "the Amorites and the Hivites"*
e   *Emendation yields "true." So Vulgate (cf. Septuagint); cf. Jer. 2.21*

As rage the mighty waters—
¹³Nations raging like massive waters!
 But He shouts at them, and they flee far away,
 Driven like chaff before winds in the hills,
 And like tumbleweed before a gale.
¹⁴At eventide, lo, terror!
 By morning, it is no more.
 Such is the lot of our despoilers,
 The portion of them that plunder us.

18

¹ᵃ⁻Ah, land in the deep shadow of wings,
 Beyond the rivers of Nubia!

²Go, swift messengers,
 To a nation ᵇ⁻far and remote,
 To a people thrust forth and away⁻ᵇ—
 A nation of gibber and chatterᶜ–
 Whose land is cut off by streams;
 ᵈ⁻Which sends out envoys by sea,
 In papyrus vessels upon the water!⁻ᵈ

³[Say this:]
 "All you who live in the world

And inhabit the earth,
 When a flag is raised in the hills, take note!
 When a ram's horn is blown, give heed!"
⁴For thus the LORD said to me:
 "I rest calm and confidentᵉ in My habitation—
 Like a scorching heat upon sprouts,
 ᶠ⁻Like a rain-cloud in the heat of reaping time."⁻ᶠ
⁵For before the harvest,ᵍ yet after the budding,
 When the blossom has hardened into berries,
 He will trim away the twigs with pruning hooks,
 And lop off the trailing branches.ʰ
⁶They shall all be left
 To the kites of the hills
 And to the beasts of the earth;
 The kites shall summer on them
 And all the beasts of the earth shall winter on
  them.

⁷In that time,
 Tribute shall be brought to the LORD of Hosts
 [From] a people far and remote,
 From a people thrust forth and away—
 A nation of gibber and chatter,
 Whose land is cut off by streams—
 At the place where the name of the LORD of
  Hosts abides,
 At Mount Zion.

19

¹The "Egypt" Pronouncement.

Mounted on a swift cloud,
 The LORD will come to Egypt;

ᵃ⁻ᵃ Or *"most sheltered land"; cf. e.g. Isa. 30.2,3; Pss. 36.8; 57.2;
  61.5*
ᵇ⁻ᵇ *Meaning of Heb uncertain*
ᶜ *Meaning of Heb uncertain; cf. 28.15 and 22.5. Biblical
  writers often characterize distant nations by their un-
  intelligible speech; cf. 33.19; Deut. 28.49; Jer. 5.15*
ᵈ⁻ᵈ *Brought down from beginning of verse for clarity. The
  Hebrew verb for "sends" agrees in gender with "nation,"
  not with "land"*
ᵉ *Cf. hibbiṭ "to rely" (Job 6.19) and mabbaṭ "reliance" (Isa.
  20.5,6)*
ᶠ⁻ᶠ *I.e. like a threat of disaster; cf. Eccl. 11.4*
ᵍ *Emendation yields "vintage"*
ʰ *Apparently a figure of speech for the Assyrians*

Egypt's idols shall tremble before Him,
And the heart of the Egyptians shall sink within
them.

²"I will incite Egyptian against Egyptian:
They shall war with each other,
Every man with his fellow,
City with city
And kingdom with kingdom.ᵃ
³Egypt shall be drained of spirit,
And I will confound its plans;
So they will consult the idols and the shades
And the ghosts and the familiar spirits.
⁴And I will place the Egyptians
At the mercy of a harsh master,
And a ruthless king shall rule them"—
Declares the Sovereign, the LORD of Hosts.

⁵Water shall fail from the seas,
Rivers dry up and be parched,
⁶Channels turn foul as they ebb,
And Egypt's canals run dry.
Reed and rush shall decay,
⁷ᵇ·And the Nile papyrus by the Nile-side·ᵇ
And everything sown by the Nile
Shall wither, blow away, and vanish.
⁸The fishermen shall lament;
All who cast lines in the Nile shall mourn,
And those who spread nets on the water shall
languish.
⁹The flax workers, too, shall be dismayed,
Both carders and weavers chagrined.ᵇ
¹⁰ᶜHer foundations shall be crushed,
And all who make dams shall be despondent.

¹¹Utter fools are the nobles of Tanis;
The sagest of Pharaoh's advisors

[Have made] absurd predictions.
How can you say to Pharaoh,
"I am a scion of sages,
A scion of Kedemite kingsᵈ"?
¹²Where, indeed, are your sages?
Let them tell you, let them discover
What the LORD of Hosts has planned against
Egypt.
¹³The nobles of Tanis have been fools,
The nobles of Memphis deluded;
Egypt has been led astray
By the chiefs of her tribes.
¹⁴The LORD has mixed within her
A spirit of distortion,
Which shall lead Egypt astray in all her under-
takings
As a vomiting drunkard goes astray;
¹⁵Nothing shall be achieved in Egypt
By either head or tail,
Palm branch or reed.ᵉ

¹⁶ In that day, the Egyptians shall be like women,
trembling and terrified because the LORD of Hosts
will raise His hand against them. ¹⁷And the land
of Judah shall also be the dread of the Egyptians;
they shall quake whenever anybody mentions it
to them, because of what the LORD of Hosts is
planning against them. ¹⁸In that day, there shall
be severalᶠ towns in the land of Egypt speaking

a   *I.e. the various districts of Egypt, which in Isaiah's time*
    were governed by hereditary princes
b-b *Meaning of Heb uncertain*
c   *Meaning of verse uncertain; emendation yields*
        "Her drinkers shall be dejected,
        And all her brewers despondent"
d   *Or "advisors." The wisdom of the Kedemites was prover-*
    bial; cf. I Ki. 5.10
e   *I.e. a man of either high or low station; cf. 9.13, 14*
f   *Lit. "five"*

the language of Canaan and swearing loyalty to the LORD of Hosts; *g-each one-g* shall be called Town of Heres.*h*

19 In that day, there shall be an altar to the LORD inside the land of Egypt and a pillar to the LORD at its border.*i* 20They shall serve as a symbol and and a reminder of the LORD of Hosts in the land of Egypt, so that when [the Egyptians] cry out to the LORD against oppressors, He will send them a savior and champion to deliver them. 21For the LORD will make Himself known to the Egyptians, and the Egyptians shall acknowledge the LORD in that day, and they shall serve [Him] with sacrifice and oblation and shall make vows to the LORD and fulfill them. 22The LORD will first afflict and then heal the Egyptians; when they turn back to the LORD, He will respond to their entreaties and heal them.

23 In that day, there shall be a highway from Egypt to Assyria. The Assyrians shall join with the Egyptians and Egyptians with the Assyrians, and then the Egyptians together with the Assyrians shall serve [the LORD].

24In that day, Israel shall be a third partner with Egypt and Assyria as a blessing*j* on earth; 25for the LORD of Hosts will bless them, saying, "Blessed be My people Egypt, My handiwork Assyria, and My very own Israel."

g-g Or "one"
h Meaning uncertain. Many Heb mss. read ḥeres, "sun," which may refer to Heliopolis, i.e. Sun City, in Egypt. Targum. "Beth Shemesh" (cf. Jer. 43.13) has the same meaning
i As a symbol of God's sovereignty over Egypt
j I.e. a standard by which blessing is invoked; cf. Gen. 12.2 with note

a An Assyrian title meaning "General"; cf. II Kings 18.17
b Lit. "At that time,"
a-a Emendation yields "The 'From the Desert' Pronouncement," agreeing with the phrase further on in the verse

20

1It was the year that the Tartan*a* came to Ashdod —being sent by King Sargon of Assyria—and attacked Ashdod and took it. 2Previously,*b* the LORD had spoken to Isaiah son of Amoz, saying, "Go, untie the sackcloth from your loins and take your sandals off your feet," which he had done, going naked and barefoot. 3And now the LORD said, "It is a sign and a portent for Egypt and Nubia. Just as My servant Isaiah has gone naked and barefoot for three years, 4so shall the king of Assyria drive off the captives of Egypt and the exiles of Nubia, young and old, naked and barefoot and with bared buttocks—to the shame of Egypt! 5And they shall be dismayed and chagrined because of Nubia their hope and Egypt their boast. 6In that day, the dwellers of this coastland shall say, 'If this could happen to those we looked to, to whom we fled for help and rescue from the king of Assyria, how can we ourselves escape?' "

21

1The *a-*"Desert of the Sea" Pronouncement.*-a*

Like the gales
That race through the Negeb,
It comes from the desert,
The terrible land.
2A harsh prophecy

Has been announced to me:
"The betrayer is *b*-betraying,
The ravager ravaging.-*b*
Advance, Elam!
Lay siege, Media!
c-I have put an end
To all her sighing."-*c*

3Therefore my loins
 Are seized with trembling;
 I am gripped by pangs
 Like a woman in travail,
 Too anguished to hear,
 Too frightened to see.
4My mind is confused,
 I shudder in panic.
 My night of pleasure
 He has turned to terror:
5"Set the table!"
 To "Let the watchman watch!"
 "Eat and drink!"
 To "Up, officers! grease*d* the shields!"

6For thus my Lord said to me:
 "Go, set up a sentry;
 Let him announce what he sees.
7He will see mounted men,
 Horsemen in pairs—
 Riders on asses,
 Riders on camels—
 And he will listen closely,
 Most attentively."
8And *e*-[like] a lion he-*e* called out:
 f-"On my Lord's lookout-*f* I stand
 Ever by day,
 And at my post I watch

Every night.
9And there they come, mounted men—
 Horsemen in pairs!"
 Then he spoke up and said,
 "Fallen, fallen is Babylon,
 And all the images of her gods
 Have crashed to the ground!"
10*g*-My threshing, the product of my threshing
     floor:-*g*
 What I have heard from the LORD of Hosts,
 The God of Israel—
 That I have told to you.

11The "Dumah"*h* Pronouncement.

 A call comes to me from Seir:
 "Watchman, what of the night?
 Watchman, what of the night?"
12The watchman replied,
 "Morning came, and so did night.
 If you would inquire, inquire.
 Come back again."

13The "In the Steppe" Pronouncement.

 In the scrub, in the steppe, you will lodge,
 O caravans of the Dedanites!
14Meet the thirsty with water,
 You who dwell in the land of Tema,
 Greet the fugitive with bread.

b-b *Emendation yields "betrayed . . . ravaged"; cf. 33.1*
c *Emendation yields "Put an end to all her merrymaking!"*
d *Emendation yields "grasp"*
e-e *Ms. 1QIs*a *reads "The watcher"*
f-f *Or "On a lookout, my lord"*
g-g *Connection of Heb uncertain*
h *Name of a people; cf. Gen. 25.14*

¹⁵For they have fled before swords:
  Before the whetted sword,
  Before the bow that was drawn,
  Before the stress of war.

¹⁶   For thus my Lord has said to me: "In another year, fixed like the years of a hired laborer, all the multitude of Kedar shall vanish; the remaining bows of Kedar's warriors shall be few in number; for the Lord, the God of Israel, has spoken.

22

¹The ᵃ⁻"Valley of Vision"⁻ᵃ Pronouncement.

ᵇWhat can have happened to you
 That you have gone, all of you, up on the roofs,
²O you who were full of tumult,
  You clamorous town,
  You city so gay?
  Your slain are not the slain of the sword
  Nor the dead of battle.ᶜ

³Your officers have all departed,
  They fled far away;
  Your survivors were all taken captive,
  ᵃ⁻Taken captive without their bows.⁻ᵃ
⁴That is why I say, "Let me be,
  I will weep bitterly.
  Press not to comfort me
  For the ruin of ᵈ⁻my poor people."⁻ᵈ

⁵For my Lord GOD of Hosts had a day
  Of tumult, and din, and confusion—
  ᵉ⁻Kir raged in the Valley of Vision,
  And Shoa on the hill;⁻ᵉ
⁶While Elam bore the quiver
  In troops of mounted men,
  And Kir bared the shield—
⁷And your choicest lowlands
  Were filled with chariots and horsemen:
  They stormed at Judah'sᶠ gateway
⁸And pressed beyond its screen.ᵍ

  You did give thought on that day
  To the arms in the Forest House,ʰ
⁹And you did take note of the many breaches
  In the City of David.
¹⁰ⁱ⁻And you collected the water of the Lower Pool;⁻ⁱ and you counted the houses of Jerusalem and pulled houses down to fortify the wall; ¹¹And you constructed a basin between the two walls for the water of the old pool.
    But you gave no thought to Him who planned it,
    You took no note of Him who designed it long before.
¹²My Lord GOD of Hosts summoned on that day
  To weeping and lamenting,
  To tonsuring and girding with sackcloth.

a-a Meaning of Heb uncertain
b   Vv. 1-3 describe a scene of mourning to take place in Jerusalem in the near future. In the ancient Near East, public weeping took place on the low flat roofs as well as in the streets and squares; cf. above, 15.3; Jer. 48.38
c   I.e. executed, instead of dying in battle
d-d Lit. "the young woman, my people"
e-e Meaning of Heb uncertain. On Kir see II King 16.9; Amos 1.5; 9.7; on Shoa see Ezek. 23.23
f   Brought up from 8a for clarity
g   Judah's gateway is the upper course of the Valley of Elah. The screen is the fortress Azekah at the mouth of the gateway. Azekah was captured by the Assyrians in 712 B.C.E.
h   See 1 Kings 7.2-5; 10.16-17; 14.26-27
i-i Perhaps to be read after v. 11a

13Instead, there was rejoicing and merriment,
Killing of cattle and slaughtering of sheep,
Eating of meat and drinking of wine:
"Eat and drink, for tomorrow we die."
14Then the LORD of Hosts revealed Himself to my
ears:
"This iniquity shall never be forgiven you
Until you die," said my Lord GOD of Hosts.

15   Thus said my Lord GOD of Hosts: Go in to
see that steward, that Shebna, in charge of the
palace: 16What have you here, and whom have
you here, that you have hewn out a tomb for
yourself here?—O you who have hewn your*j*
tomb on high; O you who have hollowed out for
yourself*j* an abode in the cliff! 17The LORD is
about to shake you *k*-severely, fellow,-*k* and then
wrap you around Himself.*l* 18Indeed, He will
wind you about him *m*-as a headdress, a turban.-*m*
Off to a broad land! There shall you die, and
there shall be the *n*-chariots bearing your body,-*n*
O shame of your master's house! 19For I will hurl
you from your station and you shall be torn down
from your stand.

20   And in that day, I will summon My servant
Eliakim son of Hilkiah, 21and I will invest him
with your tunic, gird him with your sash, and
deliver your authority into his hand; and he shall
be a father to the inhabitants of Jerusalem and
the men of Judah. 22I will place the keys of
David's palace on his shoulders; and what he un-
locks none may shut, and what he locks none may
open. 23I will fix him as a peg in a firm place,*o*
24on which all the substance of his father's*p* house-
hold shall be hung: *a*-the sprouts and the leaves-*a*—
all the small vessels, from bowls to all sorts of jars.

*o*He shall be a seat of honor to his father's*p* house-
hold.
25   *q*In that day—declares the LORD of Hosts—the
peg fixed in a firm place shall give way: it shall be
cut down and shall fall, and the weight it sup-
ports shall be destroyed. For it is the LORD who
has spoken.

23

1*a*The "Tyre" Pronouncement.

Howl, you ships of Tarshish!
For havoc has been wrought, not a house is left;
As they came from the land of Kittim,
This was revealed to them.

2Moan, you coastland dwellers,
You traders of Sidon!
You*b* were filled with men who crossed the sea.
3Over many waters
Your*c* revenue came:
From the trade of nations,
From the grain of Shihor,
The harvest of the Nile.
4Be ashamed, O Sidon!
For the sea—this stronghold of the sea—declares,

j   Heb "his," "himself"
k-k Emendation yields "as a garment is shaken out"
l   I.e. and walk off with you; cf. Jer. 43.12
m-m Emendation yields "as a turban is wound about"
n-n Emendation yields "abode(cf. v. 16)of your body"(cf. 10.16)
o   V. 23b is brought down to the end of v. 24 for clarity
p   Emendation yields "master's"; cf. v. 18 end
q   Apparently continues v. 19

a   The meaning of much of vv. 1-3 is uncertain
b   I.e. Sidon
c   Heb "her"

d-"I am as one who has-*d* never labored,
Never given birth,
Never raised youths
Or reared maidens!"
⁵When the Egyptians heard it, they quailed
As when they heard about Tyre.

⁶Pass on to Tarshish—
Howl, you coastland dwellers!
⁷Was such your merry city
In former times, of yore?
Did her feet carry her off
To sojourn far away?
⁸Who was it that planned this
For crown-wearing Tyre,
Whose merchants were nobles,
Whose traders the world honored?
⁹The Lᴏʀᴅ of Hosts planned it—
To defile all glorious beauty,
To shame all the honored of the world.

¹⁰*e*-Traverse your land like the Nile,
Fair Tarshish;-*e*
This is a harbor*f* no more.

¹¹'Twas the Lᴏʀᴅ poised His arm o'er the sea

And made kingdoms quake;
'Twas He decreed destruction
For Phoenicia's*g* strongholds,
¹²And said,
"You shall be gay no more,
O plundered one, Fair Maiden Sidon.
Up, cross over to Kittim—
Even there you shall have no rest."

¹³*h*Behold the land of Chaldea—
This is the people that has ceased to be.
Assyria, which founded it for ships,
Which raised its watchtowers,
Erected its ramparts,
Has turned it into a ruin.

¹⁴Howl, O ships of Tarshish,
For your stronghold is destroyed!

¹⁵   In that day, Tyre shall remain forgotten for
seventy years, equaling the lifetime of one king.
After a lapse of seventy years, it shall go with
Tyre as with the harlot in the ditty:

¹⁶Take a lyre, go about the town,
    Harlot long forgotten;
Sweetly play, sing many songs,
    To bring you back to mind.

¹⁷   For after a lapse of seventy years, the Lᴏʀᴅ
will take note of Tyre, and she shall resume her
i-"fee-taking" and "play the harlot-*i*" with all the
kingdoms of the world, on the face of the earth.
¹⁸But her profits and "hire" shall be consecrated to
the Lᴏʀᴅ. They shall not be treasured or stored;
rather shall her profits go to those who abide

d-d *Lit. "I have"*
e-e *Meaning of Heb uncertain. Emendation yields*
        "Pass on to the land of Kittim,
        You ships of Tarshish"
f   *Meaning of Heb uncertain; taking* mezaḥ *as a by-form of*
        maḥoz: cf. Ps. 107.30
g   *Heb "Canaan's"*
h   *Meaning of verse uncertain. Emendation yields*
        "The land of Kittim itself—
        Which the Sidonian people founded,
        Whose watchtowers they raised,
        Whose citadels they erected—
        Exists no more;
        Assyria has turned it into a ruin"
i-i *I.e. "trading . . . trade"*

before the Lord, that they may eat their fill and clothe themselves elegantly.

24

¹Behold,
 The Lord will strip the earth bare,
 And lay it waste,
 And twist its surface,
 And scatter its inhabitants.
²Layman and priest shall fare alike,
 Slave and master,
 Handmaid and mistress,
 Buyer and seller,
 Lender and borrower,
 Creditor and debtor.
³The earth shall be bare, bare;
 It shall be plundered, plundered;
 For it is the Lord who spoke this word.

⁴The earth is withered, sear;
 The world languishes, it is sear;
 ᵃ⁻The most exalted people of the earth⁻ᵃ languish.
⁵For the earth was defiled
 Under its inhabitants;
 Because they transgressed teachings,
 Violated laws,
 Broke the ancient covenant.ᵇ
⁶That is why a curse consumes the earth,
 And its inhabitants pay the penalty;
 That is why earth's dwellers have dwindled,
 And but few men are left.

⁷The new wine fails,
 The vine languishes;
 And all the merry-hearted sigh.
⁸Stilled is the merriment of timbrels,
 Ended the clamor of revelers,
 Stilled the merriment of lyres.
⁹They drink their wine without song;
 Liquor tastes bitter to the drinker.
¹⁰Towns are broken,ᶜ empty;
 Every house is shut, none enters;
¹¹Even over wine, a cry goes up in the streets:
 The sun has set on all joy,
 The gladness of the earth is banished.
¹²Desolation is left in the town
 And the gate is battered to ruins.

¹³For thus shall it be among the peoples
 In the midst of the earth:
 As when the olive tree is beaten out,
 Like gleanings when the vintage is over.
¹⁴These shall lift up their voices,
 Exult in the majesty of the Lord.
 They shall shout from the sea:
¹⁵Therefore, honor the Lord with lights
 In the coastlands of the sea—
 The name of the Lord, the God of Israel.
¹⁶From the end of the earth
 We hear singing:
 Glory to the righteous!
 ᵈ⁻And I said:⁻ᵈ
 ᵉ⁻I waste away! I waste away! Woe is me!
 The faithless have acted faithlessly;

---

a-a *Change of vocalization yields "both sky and earth"*
b *I.e. the moral law which is binding on all men (cf. Gen. 9.4-6)*
c *Emendation yields "left"*
d-d *Change of vocalization yields "They shall say"*

The faithless have broken faith!⁻ᵉ

¹⁷ᶠ⁻Terror, and pit, and trap⁻ᶠ
  Upon you who dwell on earth!
¹⁸He who flees at the report of the terror
  Shall fall into the pit;
  And he who climbs out of the pit
  Shall be caught in the trap.
  For sluices are opened on high,
  And earth's foundations tremble.

¹⁹The earth is breaking, breaking;
  The earth is crumbling, crumbling.
  The earth is tottering, tottering;
²⁰The earth is swaying like a drunkard;
  It is rocking to and fro like a hut.
  Its iniquity shall weigh it down,
  And it shall fall, to rise no more.

²¹In that day, the LORD shall punish
  The host of heaven in heaven
  And the kings of the earth on earth.
²²They shall be gathered in a dungeon
  As captives are gathered;
  And shall be locked up in a prison.
  But after many days they shall be remembered.

²³Then the moon shall be ashamed,
  And the sun shall be abashed.

e-e *Meaning of Heb uncertain. Emendation yields*
        "Villain [Arabic razîl], foolish villain!
        The faithless who acted faithlessly
        Have been betrayed in turn"
f-f *Heb paḥad wa-paḥath, wa-paḥ*

a   *See 9.5, with note*
b   *Emendation yields "arrogant men"*
c   *Meaning of Heb uncertain*
d   *Meaning of Heb uncertain. Emendation yields, "rainstorm";*
        cf. 4d
e   *I.e. the Holy Land, as in 11.9; 14.25; 57.13*

For the LORD of Hosts will reign
On Mount Zion and in Jerusalem,
And the Presence will be revealed to His elders.

25

¹O LORD, You are my God;
  I will extol You, I will praise Your name.
  For You planned graciousnessᵃ of old,
  Counsels of steadfast faithfulness.

²For You have turned a city into a stone heap,
  A walled town into a ruin,
  The citadel of strangersᵇ into rubble,ᶜ
  Never to be rebuilt.
³Therefore a fierce people must honor You,
  A city of cruel nations must fear You.
⁴For You have been a refuge for the poor man,
  A shelter for the needy man in his distress—
  Shelter from rainstorm, shade from heat.
  When the fury of tyrants was like a winterᶜ
      rainstorm,
⁵The rage of strangersᵇ like heat in the desert,
  You subdued the heat with the shade of clouds,
  The singingᵈ of the tyrants was vanquished.

⁶The LORD of Hosts will make on this mountᵉ
  For all the peoples
  A banquet of ᶜrich viands,
  A banquet of choice wines—
  Of rich viands seasoned with marrow,
  Of choice winesᶜ well refined.

7And He will destroy on this mount*e* the shroud
That is drawn over the faces of all the peoples
And the covering that is spread
Over all the nations:
8He will destroy death*f* forever.
My Lord God will wipe the tears away
From all faces
And will put an end to the reproach of *g-*His
    people*-g*
Over all the earth—
For it is the Lord who has spoken.

9In that day they shall say:
This is our God;
We trusted in Him, and He delivered us.
This is the Lord, in whom we trusted;
Let us rejoice and exult in His deliverance!

10For the hand of the Lord shall descend
Upon this mount,*e*
And Moab*h* shall be trampled under Him
As straw is threshed to bits at Madmenah.*i*
11Then He will spread out His hands in their home-
    land,*j*
As a swimmer spreads His hands out to swim,
And He will humble their pride
Along with *k-*the emblems of their power.*-k*
Yea, the secure fortification of their*l* walls
He will lay low and humble,
Will raze to the ground, to the very dust.

26

1In that day, this song shall be sung
In the land of Judah:

Ours is a mighty city;
He makes victory our inner and outer wall.
2Open the gates, and let
A righteous nation enter,
[A nation] that keeps faith.
3The confident mind You guard in safety,
In safety because it trusts in You.

4Trust in the Lord for ever and ever,
For in Yah the Lord you have an everlasting
    Rock.
5For He has brought low those who dwelt high
    up,
Has humbled the secure city,
Humbled it to the ground,
Leveled it with the dust—
6To be trampled underfoot,
By the feet of the needy,
By the soles of the poor.

7The path is level for the righteous man;
O Just One, You make smooth the course of the
    righteous.

8For Your just ways, O Lord, we look to You;
We long for the name by which You are called.
9At night I yearn for You with all my being,

e   I.e. the Holy Land, as in 11.9; 14.25; 57.13
f   Apparently an allusion to the mass killings committed by
    the Assyrians; cf. 10.7; 14.20
g-g Emendation yields "peoples"
h   Emendation yields "Assyria"; cf. 14.25
i   A village near Jerusalem; see 10.31. Emendation yields "As
    straw gets shredded in the threshing"
j   Lit. "midst"
k-k Meaning of Heb uncertain. Emendation yields "their cita-
    dels"; cf. the next verse
l   Heb "your"

I seek You with all *the spirit within me.*
For when Your judgments are wrought on earth,
The inhabitants of the world learn righteousness.
¹⁰But when the scoundrel is spared, he learns not
   righteousness;
In a place of integrity, he does wrong—
He ignores the majesty of the LORD.

¹¹O LORD!
They see not Your hand exalted.
Let them be shamed as they behold
Your zeal for Your people
And fire consuming Your adversaries.
¹²ᵇO LORD!
May You appoint well-being for us,
Since You have also requited all our misdeeds.

¹³O LORD our God!
Lords other than You possessed us,
But only Your name shall we utter.
¹⁴They are dead, they can never live;
Shades, they can never rise;
Of a truth, You have dealt with them and wiped
   them out,
Have put an end to all mention of them.
¹⁵ᶜWhen You added to the nation, O LORD,
When You added to the nation,
Extending all the boundaries of the land,
You were honored.
¹⁶O LORD! In their distress, they sought You;

Your chastisement reduced them
To anguished*d* whispered prayer.
¹⁷Like a woman with child
Approaching childbirth,
Writhing and screaming in her pangs,
So are we become because of You, O LORD.
¹⁸We were with child, we writhed—
It is as though we had given birth to wind;
We have won no victory on earth;
The inhabitants of the world have not *come to
   life!*
¹⁹Oh, let Your dead revive!
Let corpses* arise!
Awake and shout for joy,
You who dwell in the dust!—
For Your dew is like the dew on fresh growth;
You make the land of the shades *come to life.*

²⁰Go, my people, enter your chambers,
And lock your doors behind you.
Hide but a little moment,
Until the indignation passes.
²¹For lo!
The LORD shall come forth from His place
To punish the dwellers of the earth
For their iniquity;
And the earth shall disclose its bloodshed
And shall no longer conceal its slain.

a-a *Emendation yields "my spirit in the morning"*
b   *Meaning of verse uncertain*
c   *Meaning of vv. 15-16 uncertain*
d   *Lit. "anguish"; taking* ṣaqun *as a noun formed like* zadon
     and sason
e-e *Meaning of Heb uncertain*
f   *Grammar of Heb unclear*

27

¹In that day the LORD will punish,
With His great, cruel, mighty sword,

Leviathan the Elusive^a Serpent,—
Leviathan the Twisting^a Serpent—
And He will slay the Dragon of the sea.^b

²In that day,
They shall sing of it:^c
^{d-}"Vineyard of Delight."^{-d}
³I the Lord keep watch over it,
I water it every moment;
^{e-}That no harm may befall it, ^{-e}
I watch it night and day.
⁴There is no anger in Me:
^{a-}If one offers Me thorns and thistles,
I will march to battle against him,
And set all of them on fire.^{-a}
⁵But if he holds fast to My refuge,
^{a-}He makes Me his friend;
He makes Me his friend.^{-a}

⁶In days to come Jacob shall strike root,
Israel shall sprout and blossom,
And the face of the world
Shall be covered with fruit.

⁷Was he beaten as his beater has been?
Did he suffer such slaughter as his slayers?
^{8f-}Assailing them^{-f} with fury unchained,
His pitiless blast bore them off
On a day of gale.

^{9g}Assuredly, by this alone
Shall Jacob's sin be purged away;
This is the only price
For removing his guilt:
That he make all the altar-stones

Like shattered blocks of chalk—
With no sacral pole left standing,
Nor any incense altar.
¹⁰Thus fortified cities lie desolate,
Homesteads deserted, forsaken like a wilderness;
There calves graze, there they lie down
^{h-}And consume its boughs.
¹¹When its crown is withered, they break;^{-h}
Women come and make fires with them.
For they are a people without understanding;
That is why
Their Maker will show them no mercy,
Their Creator will deny them grace.

¹²   And in that day, the Lord will beat out [the peoples like grain] from the channel of the Euphrates to the Wadi of Egypt; and you shall be picked up one by one, O children of Israel!

¹³   And in that day, a great ram's horn shall be sounded; and the strayed who are in the land of Assyria and the expelled who are in the land of Egypt shall come and worship the Lord on the holy mount, in Jerusalem.

a   *Meaning of Heb uncertain*
b   *The monster which the Lord vanquished of old (cf. Isa. 51.9; Ps. 74.13-14) was the embodiment of chaos; here it stands for the forces of evil in the present world*
c   *Apparently the earth; cf. 26.21*
d-d *So some mss. (cf. Amos 5.11); other mss. and editions have "wine"*
e-e *Meaning of Heb uncertain; emendation yields "My eye is open upon it:"*
f-f *Lit. "Striving with her"; meaning of verse uncertain*
g   *This verse might read more logically before v. 6; the thought of vv. 7-8, dealing with the punishment of Israel's enemies, is continued in vv. 10-11*
h-h *Meaning of Heb uncertain. Emendation yields "Or like a terebinth whose boughs Break when its crown is withered"*

28

¹Ah, the proud crowns of the drunkards of
  Ephraim,
Whose glorious beauty is but wilted flowers
On the heads of men bloated*ᵃ* with rich food,
Who are overcome by wine!

²Lo, my Lord has something strong and mighty,
Like a storm of hail,
A shower of pestilence.
Something like a storm of massive, torrential rain*ᵇ*
Shall be hurled with force to the ground.
³Trampled underfoot shall be
The proud crowns of the drunkards of Ephraim,
⁴The wilted flowers—
On the heads of men bloated*ᵇ* with rich food—
That are his glorious beauty.
They shall be like an early fig
Before the fruit harvest;
Whoever sees it devours it
While it is still *ᶜin his hand.ᶜ*

⁵ In that day, the LORD of Hosts shall become a
crown of beauty and a diadem of glory for the
remnant of His people,⁶ and a spirit of judgment
for him who sits in judgment and of valor for
those who repel attacks at the gate.

⁷But these are also muddled by wine

And dazed by liquor:
Priest and prophet
Are muddled by liquor;
They are confused by wine,
They are dazed by liquor;
They are muddled in their visions,
They stumble in judgment.
⁸Yea, all tables are covered
With vomit and filth,
So that no space is left.

⁹ᵈ"To whom would he give instruction?
To whom expound a message?
To those newly weaned from milk,
Just taken away from the breast?
¹⁰That same mutter upon mutter,
Murmur upon murmur,
Now here, now there!"

¹¹ Truly, as one who speaks to that people in a
stammering jargon and an alien tongue ¹²is he
who declares to them, "This is the resting place,
let the weary rest;*ᵉ* this is the place of repose."
They refuse to listen. ¹³To them the word of the
LORD is

"Mutter upon mutter,
Murmur upon murmur,
Now here, now there."
And so they will march,*ᶠ*
But they shall fall backward,
And be injured and snared and captured.

¹⁴Hear now the word of the LORD,
You men of mockery,
*ᵍ*Who govern that people*ᵍ*

ᵇ *Ge is contracted from* ge'e; *cf. Ibn Ezra*
ᵃ *Lit. "water"*
ᶜ⁻ᶜ *Emendation yields "on the bough"*
ᵈ *This is the drunkards' reaction to Isaiah's reproof*
ᵉ *I.e. do not embark on any political adventure at this time*
ᶠ *I.e. embark on the political adventure*
ᵍ⁻ᵍ *Or "composers of taunt-verses for that people"*

In Jerusalem!

¹⁵For you have said,
"We have made a covenant with Death,
Concluded a pact with Sheol.
When the sweeping flood passes through,
It shall not reach us;
For we have made falsehood our refuge,
Taken shelter in treachery."

¹⁶Assuredly,
Thus said the Lord GOD:
"Behold, I will found in Zion,
Stone by stone,
ʰ⁻A tower of precious cornerstones,⁻ʰ
Exceedingly firm;
He who trusts need not fear.

¹⁷But I will apply judgment as a measuring line
And retributionⁱ as weights;ʲ
And hail shall sweep away the refuge of false-
hood,
And flood-waters carry off your shelter.

¹⁸Your covenant with Death shall be annulled,
Your pact with Sheol shall not endure;
When the sweeping flood passes through,
You shall be its victims.

¹⁹It shall catch you
Every time it passes through;
It shall pass through every morning,
Every day and every night.
And horror alone shall be
The message there is to expound."

²⁰The couch is too short for stretching out,
And the cover too narrow for curling up!

²¹For the LORD will arise
As on the hill of Perazim,

He will rouse Himself
As in the vale of Gibeon,
To do His work—
Strange is His work!—
And to perform His task—
Astounding is His task!ᵏ

²²Therefore, refrain from mockery,
Lest your bonds be tightened.
For I have heard a decree of destruction
From my Lord GOD of Hosts
Against all the land.

²³Give diligent ear to my words,
Attend carefully to what I say.

²⁴Does he who plows to sow
Plow all the time,
Breaking up and furrowing his land?

²⁵When he has smoothed its surface,
Does he not rather broadcast black cumin
And scatter cumin,
Or set wheat in a row,ˡ
Barley in a strip,
And emmer in a patch?

²⁶For He teaches him the right manner,
His God instructs him.

²⁷So, too, black cumin is not threshed with a threshing-board,
Nor is the wheel of a threshing sledge rolled over
cumin;

h-h *Grammar and meaning uncertain*
i   *As in 1.27; 5.16; 10.22*
j   *I.e. I will make judgment and retribution My plan of action;
      cf. 34.11; II Ki. 21.13*
k   *Instead of giving victory, as at Baal-perazim and Gibeon
      (cf. II Sam. 5.19-25; I Chr. 14.9-16), He will inflict punish-
      ment*
l   *In some Near Eastern countries, wheat is actually planted
      rather than scattered*

But black cumin is beaten out with a stick
And cumin with a rod.
²⁸It is cereal that is crushed.*ᵐ*
For *ⁿ*even if*ⁿ* he threshes it thoroughly,
And the wheel of his sledge, *ᵒ*and his horses,
   overwhelm it.*ᵒ*
He does not crush it.
²⁹That, too, is ordered by the Lᴏʀᴅ of Hosts;
His counsel is unfathomable,
His wisdom marvelous.

29

¹"Ah, Ariel,*ᵃ* Ariel,
City where David camped!
Add year to year,
Let festivals come in their cycles—
²And I will harass Ariel,
And there shall be sorrow and sighing.
*ᵇ*She shall be to Me like Ariel,*ᵇ*
³And I will camp against you *ᶜ*round about;*ᶜ*
I will lay siege to you *ᵇ*with a mound,*ᵇ*
And I will set up siegeworks against you.
⁴And you shall speak from lower than the ground,
Your speech shall be humbler than the sod;
Your speech shall sound like a ghost's from the
   ground,
Your voice shall chirp from the sod.

m   *Emendation yields "threshed"*
n-n *Taking* lo *as equivalent to* lu
o-o *Meaning of Heb uncertain*

a   *A poetic name of Jerusalem; cf. 33.7*
b-b *Meaning of Heb uncertain*
c-c *Meaning of Heb uncertain; Septuagint reads "like David"*
d   *Manuscript 1QIsᵃ reads "haughty men"*

⁵And like fine dust shall be
The multitude of *ᵈ*your strangers;*ᵈ*
And like flying chaff,
The multitude of tyrants."

And suddenly, in an instant,
⁶She shall be remembered of the Lᴏʀᴅ of Hosts
With roaring, and shaking, and deafening noise,
Storm, and tempest, and blaze of consuming fire.
⁷Then, like a dream, a vision of the night,
Shall be the multitude of nations
That war upon Ariel,
And all her besiegers, and the siegeworks against
   her,
And those who harass her.
⁸Like one who is hungry
And dreams he is eating,
But wakes to find himself empty;
And like one who is thirsty
And dreams he is drinking,
But wakes to find himself faint
And utterly parched—
So shall be all the multitude of nations
That war upon Mount Zion.

⁹Act stupid and be stupified!
Act blind and be blinded!
(They are drunk, but not from wine,
They stagger, but not from liquor.)
¹⁰For the Lᴏʀᴅ has spread over you
A spirit of deep sleep,
And has shut your eyes, the prophets,
And covered your heads, the seers;
¹¹So that all prophecy has been to you
Like the words of a sealed document.

If it is handed to one who can read and he is

asked to read it, he will say, "I can't, because it is sealed"; 12and if the document is handed to one who cannot read and he is asked to read it, he will say, "I can't read."

13My Lord said:
Because that people has approached [Me] with
    its mouth
And honored Me with its lips,
But has kept its heart far from Me,
And its worship of Me has been
A commandment of men, learned by rote—
14Truly, I shall further baffle that people
With bafflement upon bafflement;
And the wisdom of its wise shall fail,
And the prudence of its prudent shall vanish.

15Ha! Those who would hide their plans
Deep from the LORD!
Who do their work in dark places
And say, "Who sees us, who takes note of us?"
16e-How perverse of you!
Should the potter be accounted as the clay?-e
Should what is made say of its Maker,
"He did not make me,"
And what is formed say of Him who formed it,
f-"He did not understand?"-f
17Surely, in a little while,
Lebanon will be transformed into farm land,
And farm land accounted as mere brush.
18In that day, the deaf shall hear even written
    words,
And the eyes of the blind shall see
Even in darkness and obscurity.
19Then the humble shall have increasing joy
    through the LORD,

And the neediest of men shall exult
In the Holy One of Israel.
20For the tyrant shall be no more,
The scoffer shall cease to be,
And those diligent for evil shall be wiped out,
21Who made men fail in lawsuits,
Laying a snare for the arbiter at the gate,
And wronging by falsehood
Him who was in the right.
22   Assuredly, thus said the LORD, who redeemed Abraham, to the House of Jacob:
No more shall Jacob be shamed,
No longer his face grow pale.

23   For when he—that is, his children—behold what My hands have wrought in his midst, they will hallow My name.

Men will hallow the Holy One of Jacob
And stand in awe of the God of Israel.
And the confused shall acquire insight
And grumblers accept instruction.

30

1Oh, disloyal sons!
    —declares the LORD—
Making plans
Against My wishes,

e-e *Meaning of first line uncertain; emendation yields
    "Should the potter be accounted
    Like the jugs or like the clay?"*
f-f *Emendation yields "did not fashion me"*

Weaving schemes
Against My will,
Thereby piling
Guilt on guilt!
²Who set out to go down to Egypt
Without asking Me,
To seek refuge with Pharaoh,
To seek shelter under the protection of Egypt.

³The refuge with Pharaoh shall result in your
    shame;
The shelter under Egypt's protection, in your
    chagrin.
⁴Though his officers are present in Zoan,ᵃ
And his messengersᵇ reach as far as Hanes,
⁵They all shall come to shame
Because of a people that does not avail them,
That is of no help or avail,
But only chagrin and disgrace.

⁶ᶜ⁻The "Beasts of the Negeb" Pronouncement.⁻ᶜ

Through a land of distress and hardship,
Of lion and roaringᵈ king-beast,
Of viper and flying seraph,ᵉ
They convey
Their wealth on the backs of asses,
Their treasures on camels' humps,
To a people of no avail.

ᵃ   *Or "Tanis"*
ᵇ   *Emendation yields "kings"; cf. 19.2 with note*
ᶜ⁻ᶜ *Meaning of Heb uncertain; emendation yields "Through the
    wasteland of the Negeb"*
ᵈ   *Meaning of Heb uncertain*
ᵉ   *See note on 14.29*
ᶠ⁻ᶠ *Meaning of Heb uncertain. Emendation yields "disgrace and
    shame"; cf. v. 5*
ᵍ   *Understanding 'ad, with Targum, as a variant of 'ed*

⁷For the help of Egypt
Shall be vain and empty.
Truly, ᶠ⁻I say of this,
"They are a threat that has ceased."⁻ᶠ

⁸Now,
Go, write it down on a tablet
And inscribe it in a record,
That it may be with them for future days,
A witnessᵍ forever.
⁹For it is a rebellious people,
Faithless children,
Children who refused to heed
The instruction of the LORD;
¹⁰Who said to the seers,
"Do not see,"
To the prophets, "Do not prophesy truth to us;
Speak to us falsehoods,
Prophesy delusions.
¹¹Leave the way!
Get off the path!
Let us hear no more
About the Holy One of Israel!"

¹²Assuredly,
Thus said the Holy One of Israel:
Because you have rejected this word,
And have put your trust and reliance
In that which is fraudulent and tortuous—
¹³Of a surety,
This iniquity shall work on you
Like a spreading breach that occurs in a lofty
    wall,
Whose crash comes sudden and swift.
¹⁴It is smashed as one smashes a pottery jug,
Ruthlessly shattered

So that no sherd is left in its breakage
To scoop coals from a brazier,
Or ladle water from a puddle.

¹⁵For thus said my Lord G<small>OD</small>,
The Holy One of Israel,
"You shall triumph by stillness and quiet;
Your victory shall come about
Through calm and confidence."
But you refused.
¹⁶"No," you declared.
"We shall flee on steeds"—
Therefore you shall flee!
"We shall ride on swift mounts"—
Therefore your pursuers shall prove swift!
¹⁷One thousand before the shout of one—
You shall flee at the shout of five;
Till what is left of you
Is like a mast on a hilltop,
Like a pole upon a mountain.

¹⁸Truly, the L<small>ORD</small> is waiting to show you grace,
Truly, He will arise to pardon you.
For the L<small>ORD</small> is a God of justice;
Happy are all who wait for Him.

¹⁹   Indeed, O People in Zion, dwellers of Jerusalem, you shall not have cause to weep. He will grant you His favor at the sound of your cry; He will respond as soon as He hears it. ²⁰My Lord will provide for you meager bread and scant water. Then your Guide will no more ^{d-}be ignored,^{-d} but your eyes will watch your Guide; ²¹and your ears will heed the direction from behind you which says, "This is the road; follow it!" whenever you deviate to the right or to the left. ²²And you will treat as unclean the silver overlay of your images and the golden plating of your idols. ^{d-}You will cast them away as something defiled, you will call them filth.^{-d}

²³   So rain shall be provided for the seed with which you sow the ground, and the bread which the ground brings forth shall be rich and fat. Your livestock, in that day, shall graze in broad pastures; ²⁴as for the cattle and the asses which till the soil, they shall partake of salted fodder that has been winnowed with shovel and fan.

²⁵   And on every high mountain and on every lofty hill, there shall appear brooks and watercourses—on a day of heavy slaughter, when towers topple. ²⁶And the light of the moon shall become like the light of the sun, and the light of the sun shall become sevenfold, like the light of the seven days, when the L<small>ORD</small> binds up His people's wounds and heals the injuries it has sustained.

²⁷Behold the ^{h-}L<small>ORD</small> Himself^{-h}
Comes from afar
In blazing wrath,
ⁱ⁻With a heavy burden—ⁱ
His lips full of fury,
His tongue like devouring fire,
²⁸And his breath like a raging torrent
Reaching halfway up the neck—
To set a misguiding yoke^j upon nations
And a misleading bridle upon the jaws of peoples,

²⁹For you, there shall be singing

d   *Meaning of Heb uncertain*
h-h   *Lit. "the name of the* L<small>ORD</small>*"*
i-i   *Presumably with a heavy load of punishment. Meaning of Heb uncertain*
j   *Interpreting* naphath *like Arabic* nāf; *meaning of line uncertain*

As on a night when a festival is hallowed;
There shall be rejoicing as when they march
With flute, *k*-with timbrels, and with lyres-*k*
To the Rock of Israel on the Mount of the Lord.

³⁰For the Lord will make His majestic voice heard
And display the sweep of His arm
In raging wrath,
In a devouring blaze of fire,
In tempest, and rainstorm, and hailstones.
³¹Truly, Assyria, who beats with the rod,
Shall be cowed by the voice of the Lord;
³²*d*-And each time the appointed staff passes by,
The Lord will bring down [His arm] upon him
And will do battle with him as he waves it.-*d*
³³The Topheth*l* has long been ready for him;
He too is destined for Melech*m*—
His fire-pit has been made both wide and deep,
With plenty of fire and firewood,
And with the breath of the Lord
Burning in it like a stream of sulfur.

31

¹Ha!
Those who go down to Egypt for help
And rely upon horses!
They have put their trust in abundance of
    chariots,
In vast numbers of riders,

And they have not turned to the Holy One of
    Israel,
Have not sought the Lord.

²But He too is wise!
He has brought on misfortune,
And has not canceled His word.
So He shall rise against the house of evildoers,
And the allies*a* of the workers of iniquity.
³For the Egyptians are man, not God,
And their horses are flesh, not spirit;
And when the Lord stretches out His arm,
The helper shall trip
And the helped one shall fall,
And both shall perish together.

⁴For thus the Lord has said to me:
As a lion—a great beast—
Growls over its prey,
And when the shepherds gather
In force against him,
Is not dismayed by their cries
Nor cowed by their noise—
So the Lord of Hosts will descend to make war
Against the mount and the hill of Zion.

⁵   Like the birds that fly, even so shall the Lord
of Hosts shield Jerusalem, shielding and saving,
protecting and rescuing.
⁶*b*-Return, O children of Israel,-*b* to Him to whom
they have been so shamefully false; ⁷for in that
day everyone will reject his idols of silver and
idols of gold, which your hands have made for
your guilt.

⁸Then Assyria shall fall,

---

k-k *Brought from v. 32 for clarity*
l   *A site near Jerusalem at which human beings were sacrificed
       by fire in periods of paganizing; see II Ki. 23.10*
m   *Cf. Moloch, Lev. 18.21; 20.2-5*

a   *Lit. "help"*
b-b *Emendation yields "Then the children of Israel shall re-
       turn"*

Not by the sword of man;
A sword not of humans shall devour him.
He shall shrivel^c before the sword,
And his young men ^{d-}pine away.^{-d}
⁹His rock shall melt with terror,
And his officers shall ^{e-}collapse from weakness^{-e}—
Declares the LORD, who has a fire in Zion,
Who has an oven in Jerusalem.^f

32

¹Behold, a king shall reign in righteousness,
And ministers shall govern with justice;
²Every one of them shall be
Like a refuge from gales,
A shelter from rainstorms;
Like brooks of water in a desert,
Like the shade of a massive rock
In a languishing land.

³Then the eyes of those who have sight shall not
be sealed,
And the ears of those who have hearing shall
listen;
⁴And the minds of the thoughtless shall attend and
note,
And the tongues of mumblers shall speak with
fluent eloquence.
⁵No more shall a villain be called noble,
Nor shall "gentleman" be said of a knave.
⁶For the villain speaks villainy
And plots treachery;

To act impiously
And to preach disloyalty against the LORD;
To leave the hungry unsatisfied
And deprive the thirsty of drink.
⁷As for the knave, his tools are knavish.
He forges plots
To destroy the poor with falsehoods
And the needy when they plead their cause.
⁸But the noble has noble intentions
And is constant in noble acts.

⁹You carefree women,
Attend, hear my words!
You confident ladies,
Give ear to my speech!
¹⁰ᵃ⁻In little more than a year,⁻ᵃ
You shall be troubled, O confident ones,
When the vintage is over
And no ingathering takes place.
¹¹Tremble, you carefree ones!
Quake, O confident ones!
Strip yourselves naked,
Put the cloth about your loins!
¹²Lament ᵇ⁻upon the breasts,⁻ᵇ
For the pleasant fields,
For the spreading grapevines;
¹³For my people's soil—
It shall be overgrown with briers and thistles—
Aye, and for all the houses of delight,
For the city of mirth.

c   *From root nss; cf. 10.18; others "flee"*
d-d *From root mss; cf. 10.18; others "become tributary"*
e-e *Cf. note c; meaning of Heb uncertain*
f   *Cf. 30.33*

a-a *Meaning of Heb uncertain*
b-b *Emendation yields "for the fields"*

¹⁴For the castle shall be abandoned,
The noisy city forsaken;
Citadel and tower shall become
ᶜ⁻Bare placesᶜ forever,
A stamping ground for wild asses,
A pasture for flocksᵈ—
¹⁵Till a spirit from on high is poured out on us,
And wilderness is transformed into farm land,
While farm land rates as mere brush.ᵉ
¹⁶Then justice shall abide in the wilderness
And righteousness shall dwell on the farm land.
¹⁷For the work of righteousness shall be peace,
And the effect of righteousness, calm and con-
fidence forever.
¹⁸Then my people shall dwell in peaceful homes,
In secure dwellings,
In untroubled places of rest.
¹⁹ᶠAnd the brush shall sink and vanish,
Even as the city is laid low.

²⁰Happy shall you be who sow by all waters,
Who ᵍ⁻send out cattle and asses to pasture.⁻ᵍ

c-c *Meaning of Heb uncertain; emendation yields "Brushland, desert"*
d *Emendation yields "onagers"; cf. Job 39.5*
e *I.e. the transformed wilderness will surpass in fertility what is now used as farm land*
f *Meaning of v. uncertain*
g-g *Lit. "let loose the feet of cattle and asses"; cf. 7.25 end*

a-a *Emendation yields "You have been our help"*
b *Heb "your spoil"*
c *Meaning of Heb uncertain. Emendation yields "booty"; cf. v. 23*
d *Taking šqq as a cognate of qšš*
e *Apparently for food; cf. Lev. 11.22*
f-f *Meaning of Heb uncertain*
g *Heb "his"*
h *So a few manuscripts; cf. 29.1*
i *I.e. Jerusalem's; cf. Salem (Heb shalem), Ps. 76.3*
j *1QIsᵃ reads "A pact"*
k-k *Emendation yields "an obligation"*

33

¹Ha, you ravager who are not ravaged,
You betrayer who have not been betrayed!
When you have done ravaging, you shall be
ravaged;
When you have finished betraying, you shall be
betrayed.

²O LORD, be gracious to us!
It is to You we have looked;
ᵃ⁻Be their armᵃ every morning,
Also our deliverance in time of stress.
³At [Your] roar peoples have fled,
Before Your majesty nations have scattered;
⁴And spoilᵇ was gathered as locusts are gathered,
Itᶜ was amassedᵈ as grasshoppers are amassed.ᵉ

⁵The LORD is exalted;
He dwells on high!
He filled Zion
With justice and righteousness.
⁶Faithfulness to ᶠ⁻Your chargeᶠ was [her] wealth,
Wisdom and devotion [her] triumph,
Reverence for the LORD—that was herᵍ treasure.

⁷Hark! The Arielitesʰ cry aloud;
Shalom'sⁱ messengers weep bitterly.
⁸Highways are desolate,
Wayfarers have ceased.
A covenant has been renounced,
Citiesʲ rejected
ᵏ⁻Mortal manᵏ despised.
⁹The land is wilted and withered;

Lebanon disgraced and moldering,
Sharon is become like a desert,
And Bashan and Carmel are stripped bare.

10"Now I will arise," says the LORD,
"Now I will exalt Myself, now raise Myself high.
11You shall conceive hay,
Give birth to straw;
My*l* breath will devour you like fire.
12Peoples shall be burnings of lime,*m*
Thorns cut down that are set on fire.
13Hear, you who are far, what I have done;
You who are near, note My might."

14Sinners in Zion are frightened,
The godless are seized with trembling:
"Who of us can dwell with the devouring fire:
Who of us can dwell with the never-dying
blaze?"
15He who walks in righteousness,
Speaks uprightly,
Spurns profit from fraudulent dealings,
Waves away a bribe, instead of grasping it,
Stops his ears against listening to infamy,
Shuts his eyes against looking at evil—
16Such a one shall dwell in lofty security,
With inaccessible cliffs for his stronghold,
With his food supplied
And his drink assured.

17When your eyes behold *n*a king in his beauty,*n*
When they contemplate the land round about,
18Your throat*o* shall murmur in awe,
"Where is one who could count? Where is one
who could weigh?

Where is one who could count [all these]
towers?"
19No more shall you see the barbarian folk,
The people of speech too obscure to comprehend,
So stammering of tongue that they are not understood.

20When you gaze upon Zion, our city of assembly,
Your eyes shall behold Jerusalem
As a secure homestead,
A tent not to be transported,
Whose pegs shall never be pulled up,
And none of whose ropes shall break.
21For there the LORD in His greatness shall be for us
Like a region of rivers, of broad streams,
Where no floating vessels can sail
And no mighty craft can travel—
*p-*Their*q* ropes are slack,
They cannot steady the sockets of their masts,
They cannot spread a sail.*-p*
22For the LORD shall be our ruler,
The LORD shall be our prince,
The LORD shall be our king:
He shall deliver us.
23Then *r-* shall indeed much spoil be divided,*-r*
Even the lame shall seize booty.
24And none who lives there shall say, "I am sick";
It shall be inhabited by folk whose sin has been
forgiven.

l   *Heb "your"*
m   *Emendation yields "brambles"; cf. 32.13*
n-n *Emendation yields "perfection of beauty"; cf. Ps. 50.3*
o   *As in 59.13 and elsewhere; others "heart"*
p-p *Brought up from v. 23 for clarity. The passage means that
     the Lord will render Jerusalem as inaccessible to enemies
     as if it were surrounded by an impassable sea*
q   *Heb "your"*
r-r *Meaning of Heb uncertain; emendation yields "even a blind
     man shall divide spoil"*

34

¹Approach, O nations, and listen,
 Give heed, O peoples!
 Let the earth and those in it hear;
 The world, and what it brings forth.
²For the Lord is angry at all the nations,
 Furious at all their host;
 He has doomed them, consigned them to
  slaughter.
³Their slain shall be left lying,
 And the stench of their corpses shall mount;
 And the hills shall be drenched with their blood,
⁴ᵃˑAll the host of heaven shall molder.ˑᵃ
 The heavens shall be rolled up like a scroll,
 And all their host shall wither,
 Like a leaf withering on the vine
 Or shriveled fruit on a fig tree.
⁵For My sword shall ᵇˑbe drunkˑᵇ in the sky;
 Lo, it shall come down upon Edom,
 Upon the people I have doomed,
 To wreak judgment.
⁶The Lord has a sword; it is sated with blood,
 It is gorged with fat—
 The blood of lambs and he-goats,
 The kidney fat of rams.

For the Lord holds a sacrifice in Bozrah,
 A great slaughter in the land of Edom.
⁷Wild oxen shall fall ᶜˑwith them,ˑᶜ
 Young bulls with mighty steers;
 And their land shall be drunk with blood,
 Their soil shall be saturated with fat.
⁸For it is the Lord's day of retribution,
 The year of vindication for Zion's cause.
⁹Itsᵈ streams shall be turned to pitch
 And its soil to sulfur.
 Its land shall become burning pitch,
¹⁰Night and day it shall never go out;
 Its smoke shall rise for all time.
 Through the ages it shall lie in ruins;
 Through the aeons none shall traverse it.
¹¹ᵉˑJackdaws and owlsˑᵉ shall possess it;
 Great owls and ravens shall dwell there.
 He shall measure it with a line of chaos
 And with weights of emptiness.ᶠ
¹²ᵉˑIt shall be called, "No kingdom is there,"ˑᵉ
 Its nobles and all its lords shall be nothing.
¹³Thorns shall grow up in its palaces,
 Nettles and briers in its strongholds.
 It shall be a home of jackals,
 An abode of ostriches.
¹⁴ᵍWild cats shall meet hyenas,
 Goat-demons shall greet each other;
 There too the lilithʰ shall repose
 And find herself a resting place.
¹⁵There the arrow-snake shall nest and lay eggs,
 And shall brood and hatch in its shade.
 There too the buzzards shall gather
 With one another.
¹⁶Search and read it in the scroll of the Lord:
 Not one of these shall be absent,
 Not one shall miss its fellow.

a-a *1QIsᵃ reads*
        "And the valleys shall be cleft,
        And all the hosts of heaven shall wither"
b-b *1QIsᵃ reads "be seen"; cf. Targum*
c-c *Emendation yields "with fatted calves"*
d *I.e. Edom's*
e-e *Meaning of Heb uncertain*
f *I.e. He shall plan chaos and emptiness for it; cf. Isa. 28.17;
   Lam. 2.8*
g *Most of the creatures in vv. 14-15 cannot be identified with
   certainty*
h *A kind of demon*

For His[i] mouth has spoken,
It is His spirit that has assembled them,
17And it is He who apportioned it to them by lot,
Whose hand divided it for them with the line.
They shall possess it for all time,
They shall dwell there through the ages.

35

1The arid desert shall be glad,
The wilderness shall rejoice
And shall blossom like a rose.[a]
2It shall blossom abundantly,
It shall also exult and shout.
It shall receive the glory of Lebanon,
The splendor of Carmel and Sharon.
They shall behold the glory of the LORD,
The splendor of our God.

3Strengthen the hands that are slack;
Make firm the tottering knees!
4Say to the anxious of heart,
"Be strong, fear not;
Behold your God!
Requital is coming,
The recompense of God—
He Himself is coming to give you triumph."

5Then the eyes of the blind shall be opened,
And the ears of the deaf shall be unstopped.
6Then the lame shall leap like a deer,
And the tongue of the dumb shall shout aloud;
For waters shall burst forth in the desert,
Streams in the wilderness.

7Torrid earth shall become a pool;
Parched land, fountains of water;
The home of jackals, a pasture[b];
The abode [of ostriches][c], reeds and rushes.
8And a highway shall appear there,
Which shall be called the Sacred Way.
No one unclean shall pass along it,
But it shall be for them.[d]
[e]No traveler, not even fools, shall go astray.[e]
9No lion shall be there,
No ferocious beast shall set foot on it—
These shall not be found there.
But the redeemed shall walk it;
10And the ransomed of the LORD shall return,
And come with shouting to Zion,
Crowned with joy everlasting.
They shall attain joy and gladness,
While sorrow and sighing flee.

36

1[a]In the fourteenth year of King Hezekiah, King Sennacherib of Assyria marched upon all the fortified towns of Judah and seized them. 2From Lachish, the king of Assyria sent the Rabshakeh,[b] with a large force, to Hezekiah in Jerusalem.

i   *Heb "My"*

a   *Lit. "crocus"*
b   *Meaning of Heb uncertain; emendation yields "a marsh"*
c   *Cf. 34.13*
d   *Emendation yields "for His people"*
e-e *Meaning of Heb uncertain*

a   *Chs. 36-39 occur also as II Ki. 18.13-20.19, with a number of variants, some of which will be cited here in the footnotes*
b   *An Assyrian title; cf. "Tartan," 20.1*

³[The Rabshakeh] took up a position near the conduit of the Upper Pool, by the road of the Fuller's Field; ³and Eliakim son of Hilkiah who was in charge of the palace, Shebna the secretary, and Joah son of Asaph the recorder went out to him.

⁴ The Rabshakeh said to them, "You tell Hezekiah: Thus said the Great King, the king of Assyria: ⁵What makes you so confident? I suppose*c* mere talk makes counsel and valor for war! Look, on whom are you relying, that you have rebelled against me? ⁶You are relying on Egypt, that splintered reed of a staff, which enters and punctures the palm of anyone who leans on it. That's what Pharaoh King of Egypt is like to all who rely on him. ⁷And if you are going to tell me that you're relying on the LORD your God, He is the very one whose altars and shrines Hezekiah did away with, telling Judah and Jerusalem, 'You must worship only at this altar'! ⁸Come now, make this wager with my master, the king of Assyria: I'll give you two thousand horses, if you're able to produce riders to mount them. ⁹So how could you refuse anything even to the deputy of one of my master's lesser servants, relying on Egypt for chariots and horsemen? ¹⁰And do you think I have marched against this land to destroy it without the LORD? The LORD Himself told me: Go up against that land and destroy it."

¹¹ Eliakim, Shebna, and Joah replied to the Rabshakeh, "Please, speak to your servants in Aramaic, since we understand it; do not speak to us in Judean in the hearing of the people on the wall." ¹²But the Rabshakeh replied, "Was it to your master and to you that my master sent me to speak those words? It was precisely to the men who are sitting on the wall—who will have to eat their dung and drink their urine with you." ¹³And the Rabshakeh stood and called out in a loud voice in Judean: ¹⁴"Hear the words of the Great King, the king of Assyria! Thus said the king: Don't let Hezekiah deceive you, for he will not be able to save you. ¹⁵Don't let Hezekiah make you rely on the LORD, saying: 'The LORD will surely save us; this city will not fall into the hands of Assyria!' ¹⁶Don't listen to Hezekiah. For thus said the king of Assyria: Make your peace with me and come out to me,*d* so that you may all eat from your vines and your fig trees and drink water from your cisterns ¹⁷while waiting for me to come and take you away to a land like your own, a land of bread and wine, of grain [fields] and vineyards. ¹⁸Beware of letting Hezekiah mislead you by saying, 'The LORD will save us.' Did any of the gods of the other nations save his land from the king of Assyria? ¹⁹Where were the gods of Hamath and Arpad? Where were the gods of Sepharvaim? And did they save Samaria from me? ²⁰Which among all the gods of those countries saved their countries from me, that the LORD should save Jerusalem from me?" But they were silent and did not answer him with a single word; for the king's order was: "Do not answer him."

And so Eliakim son of Hilkiah who was in charge of the palace, Shebna the secretary, and Joah son of Asaph the recorder came to Hezekiah with their clothes rent and they reported to him what the Rabshakeh had said.

c *II Ki. 18.20 "You (evidently) think"*
d *I.e. to my representative the Rabshakeh*

37

¹When King Hezekiah heard this, he rent his clothes and covered himself with sackcloth and went into the House of the Lord. ²He also sent Eliakim, who was in charge of the palace, Shebna the secretary, and the senior priests, covered with sackcloth, to the prophet Isaiah. ³They said to him, "Thus said Hezekiah: This day is a day of distress, and chastisement, and disgrace. ⁻ᵃThe babes have reached the birthstool, but the strength to give birth is lacking.⁻ᵃ ⁴Perhaps the Lord your God will take note of the words of the Rabshakeh, whom his master the king of Assyria has sent to blaspheme the living God, and will mete out judgment for the words that the Lord your God has heard—if you will offer up prayer for the surviving remnant."

⁵ When King Hezekiah's ministers came to Isaiah, ⁶Isaiah said to them, "Tell your master as follows: Thus said the Lord: Do not be frightened by the words of blasphemy against Me that you have heard from the minions of the king of Assyria. ⁷I will deludeᵇ him so that he will hear a rumor and return to his land, and I will make him fall by the sword in his land."

⁸ The Rabshakeh, meanwhile, returned and found the king of Assyria attacking Libnah, for he had heard that [the king] had left Lachish. ⁹But [the king of Assyria] learned that King Tirhakah of Nubia had come out to fight him; and when he heard it, he sent messengers to Hezekiah, saying, ¹⁰"Tell this to King Hezekiah of Judah: Do not let your God, on whom you are relying, mislead you into thinking that Jeru-

salem will not be delivered into the hands of the king of Assyria. ¹¹You have heard yourself what the kings of Assyria have done to all the lands, how they have annihilated them; and can you escape? ¹²Were the nations that my predecessorsᶜ destroyed—Gozan, Haran, Rezeph, and the Beth-edenites in Telassar—saved by their gods? ¹³Where is the king of Hamath? and the king of Arpad? and the king of Lair, Sepharvaim, Hena, and Ivvah?"

¹⁴ Hezekiah received the letter from the messengers and read it. Hezekiah then went up to the House of the Lord and spread it out before the Lord. ¹⁵And Hezekiah prayed to the Lord:

¹⁶"O Lord of Hosts, enthroned on the Cherubim! You alone are God of all the kingdoms of the earth. You made the heavens and the earth. ¹⁷O Lord, incline Your ear and hear, open Your eye and see. Hear all the words that Sennacherib has sent to blaspheme the living God! ¹⁸True, O Lord, the kings of Assyria have annihilated all the nationsᵈ and their lands ¹⁹and have committed their gods to the flames—for they are not gods, but man's handwork of wood and stone—and have destroyed them. ²⁰But now, O Lord our God, deliver us from his hands, and let all the kingdoms of the earth know that You, O Lord, alone [are God]ᵉ."

²¹ Then Isaiah son of Amoz sent this message to Hezekiah: "Thus said the Lord, the God of Israel, to whom you have prayed, concerning

---

a-a *I.e. the situation is desperate, and we are at a loss*
b   *Lit. "put a spirit in"*
c   *Lit. "fathers"*
d   *So II Ki. 19.17, and 13 mss. here*
e   *Supplied from II Ki. 19.19*

King Sennacherib of Assyria—²²this is the word
that the Lord has spoken concerning him:

Fair Maiden Zion despises you,
She mocks at you;
Fair Jerusalem shakes
Her head after you.
²³Whom have you blasphemed and reviled?
Against whom made loud your voice
And haughtily raised your eyes?
Against the Holy One of Israel!
²⁴Through your servants you have blasphemed my
    Lord.
Because you thought,
'Thanks to my vast chariotry,
It is I who have climbed the highest mountains,
To the remotest parts of Lebanon,
And have cut its loftiest cedars,
Its choicest cypresses,
And have reached its highest peak,
ᶠ·Its densest forest.·ᶠ
²⁵It is I who have drawnᵍ
And drunk abundant water.
I have dried out with the soles of my feet
All the streams of Egypt.'
²⁶Have you not heard? Of old
I planned that very thing,
I designed it long ago,
And now have fulfilled it.
And it has come to pass,

Laying fortified towns waste in desolate heaps.
²⁷Their inhabitants are helpless,
Shamed and dismayed.
They were but grass of the field
And green herbage,
Grass of the roofs ʰ·that is blasted
Before the east wind.·ʰ
²⁸I know all your stayings
And your goings and comings,
And how you have raged against Me.
²⁹Because you have raged against Me,
And your tumult has reached My ears,
I will place My hook in your nose
And My bit between your jaws;
And I will make you go back by the road
By which you came.

³⁰"And this is the sign for youⁱ: This year you eat
what grows of itself, and the next year what
springs from that, and in the third year sow and
reap and plant vineyards and eat their fruit.
³¹And the survivors of the House of Judah that
have escaped shall grow more stock below and
produce boughs above.
³²For a remnant shall come forth from Jerusalem,
Survivors from Mount Zion.
The zeal of the Lord of Hosts
Shall bring this to pass.

³³"Assuredly, thus said the Lord concerning the
king of Assyria:
He shall not enter this city;
He shall not aim an arrow at it,
Or advance upon it with a shield;
He shall not even pile up a siege mound against
    it.

f-f   Lit. "Its farm land forest"; exact meaning of Heb uncertain
g   Or "dug"; meaning of Heb uncertain
h-h So ms. 1QIsᵃ; cf. II Ki. 19.26. The usual reading in our
     passage means, literally, "and a field (?) before standing
     grain"
i   I.e. Hezekiah

34 He shall go back by the same way as he came,
   He shall not enter this city
                              —declares the LORD;
35 I will protect and save this city for My sake
   And for the sake of My servant David."

36That night^j an angel of the LORD went out and struck down one hundred and eighty five thousand in the Assyrian camp, and the following morning they were all dead corpses. 37So King Sennacherib of Assyria broke camp and retreated, and stayed in Nineveh. 38While he was worshiping in the temple of his god Nisroch, he was struck down with the sword by his sons Adrammelech and Sarezer. They fled to the land of Ararat, and his son Esarhaddon succeeded him as king.

38

1In those days Hezekiah fell dangerously ill. The prophet Isaiah son of Amoz came and said to him: "Thus said the LORD: Set your affairs in order, for you are going to die; you will not get well." 2Thereupon Hezekiah turned his face to the wall and prayed to the LORD. 3"Please, O LORD," he said, "remember how I have walked before You sincerely and wholeheartedly, and have done what is pleasing to You." And Hezekiah wept profusely.
4 Then the word of the LORD came to Isaiah:
5"Go and tell Hezekiah: Thus said the LORD, the God of your father David: I have heard your prayer, I have seen your tears. I hereby add fifteen years to your life. 6I will also rescue you and this city from the hands of the king of Assyria. I will defend this city. 7And this is the sign for you from the LORD that the LORD will do the thing which He has promised: 8I am going to make the shadow on the steps, which has descended on the ^a-dial of Ahaz^-a because of the sun, recede ten steps." And the sun['s shadow] receded ten steps, the same steps as it had descended.

9A poem by Hezekiah king of Judah when he recovered from the illness he had suffered:
10^bI had thought:
   I must depart in the middle of my days;
   I have been consigned to the gates of Sheol
   For the rest of my years.
11I thought, I shall never see Yah,^c
   Yah in the land of the living,
   Or ever behold men again
   Among those who inhabit the earth.
12My dwelling is pulled up and removed from me
   Like a tent of shepherds;
   My life is rolled up like a web
   And cut from the thrum.

   ^d-Only from daybreak to nightfall
   Was I kept whole,
13Then it was as though a lion
   Were breaking all my bones;

---

j   So II Ki. 19.35
a-a   Heb "steps." *A model of a dial with steps has been discovered in Egypt*
b   *Meaning of verse uncertain in part*
c   *I.e. visit His Temple*

I cried out until morning.
(Only from daybreak to nightfall
Was I kept whole.) *-d*
14I piped like a swift or a swallow,
I moaned like a dove,
As my eyes, all worn, looked to heaven:
"My Lord, I am in straits;
Be my surety!"

15What can I say? *d-*He promised me,*-d*
And He it is who has wrought it.
*d-*All my sleep had fled
Because of the bitterness of my soul.
16My Lord, for all that and despite it
My life-breath is revived;*-d*
You have restored me to health and revived me.
17Truly, it was for my own good
That I had such great bitterness:
You saved my life
From the pit of destruction,
For You have cast behind Your back
All my offenses.
18For it is not Sheol that praises You,
Not [the Land of] Death that extols You;
Nor do they who descend into the Pit
Hope for Your grace.
19The living, only the living
Gives thanks to You,
As I do this day;
Fathers*e* relate to children
Your acts of grace:
20"[It has pleased] the LORD to deliver us,

That is why we offer up music*f*
All the days of our lives
At the House of the LORD."

21When Isaiah said, "Let them take a cake of figs
and apply it to the rash, and he will recover,"
22Hezekiah asked, "What will be the sign that I
shall go up to the House of the LORD?"

39

1At that time, Merodach-baladan son of Baladan,
the king of Babylon, sent [envoys with] letters
and a gift to Hezekiah, for he had heard about his
illness and recovery. 2Hezekiah was pleased by
their coming, and he showed them his treasure
house—the silver, the gold, the spices, and the fragrant oil—and all his armory, and everything that
was to be found in his storehouses. There was
nothing in his palace or in all his realm that
Hezekiah did not show them. 3Then the prophet
Isaiah came to King Hezekiah. "What," he de-
manded of him, "did those men say to you?
Where have they come to you from?" "They
have come to me," replied Hezekiah, "from a far
country, from Babylon." 4Next he asked, "What
have they seen in your palace?" And Hezekiah
replied, "They have seen everything there is in
my palace. There was nothing in my storehouses
that I did not show them."
5   Then Isaiah said to Hezekiah, "Hear the word
of the LORD of Hosts: 6A time is coming when
everything in your palace, which your ancestors

d-d *Meaning of Heb uncertain*
e   *Heb singular*
f   Neginothai *is a poetic form of* neginoth

have stored up to this day, will be carried off to Babylon; nothing will be left behind, said the Lord. 7And some of your sons, your own issue, whom you will have fathered, will be taken to serve as eunuchs in the palace of the king of Babylon." 8Hezekiah declared to Isaiah, "The word of the Lord that you have spoken is good." For he thought, "It means that *a- safety is assured for*a my time."

40

1Comfort, oh comfort My people,
 Says your God.
2Speak tenderly to Jerusalem,
 And declare to her
 That her term of service is over,
 That her iniquity is expiated;
 For she has received at the hand of the Lord
 Double for all her sins.

3A voice rings out:
 "Clear in the desert
 A road for the Lord!
 Level in the wilderness
 A highway for our God!
4Let every valley be raised,
 Every hill and mount made low.
 Let the rugged ground become level
 And the ridges become a plain.
5The Presence of the Lord shall appear,
 And all flesh, as one, shall behold—
 For the mouth of the Lord has spoken."

6A voice rings out: "Proclaim!"
 *a-Another asks,*a "What shall I proclaim?"
 "All flesh is grass,
 All its goodness like flowers of the field:
7Grass withers, flowers fade
 When the breath of the Lord blows on them.
 Indeed, man is but grass:
8Grass withers, flowers fade—
 But the word of our God endures forever!"

9Ascend a lofty mountain,
 O herald of joy to Zion;
 Raise your voice with power,
 O herald of joy to Jerusalem—
 Raise it, have no fear;
 Announce to the cities of Judah:
 Behold your God!
10Behold, the Lord God comes in might,
 And His arm wins triumph for Him;
 See, His reward*b is with Him,
 His recompense before Him.
11Like a shepherd He pastures His flock:
 He gathers the lambs in His arms
 And carries them in His bosom;
 Gently He drives the mother sheep.

12Who measured the waters with the hollow of his hand,
 And gauged the skies with a span,
 And meted earth's dust with a measure,*c
 And weighed the mountains with a scale
 And the hills with a balance?

a-a Lit. "there shall be safety and faithfulness in"

a-a Manuscript 1QIsª and the Septuagint read "And I asked"
b The reward and recompense to the cities of Judah; cf. Jer. 31.14-15
c Heb shalish "third," probably a third of an ephah

¹³Who has plumbed the mind of the LORD,
  What man could tell Him His plan?
¹⁴Whom did He consult, and who taught Him,
  Guided Him in the way of right?
  Who guided Him in knowledge
  And showed Him the path of wisdom?

¹⁵The nations are but a drop in a bucket,
  Reckoned as dust on a balance;
  The very coastlands He lifts like motes.
¹⁶Lebanon is not fuel enough,
  Nor its beasts enough for sacrifice.
¹⁷All nations are as naught in His sight;
  He accounts them as less than nothing.

¹⁸To whom, then, can you liken God,
  What form compare to Him?
¹⁹The idol? A woodworker shaped it,
  And a smith overlaid it with gold,
  ᵈ⁻Forging links of silver.⁻ᵈ
²⁰As a gift, he chooses the mulberryᵉ—
  A wood that does not rot—
  Then seeks a skillful woodworker
  To make a firm idol,
  That will not topple.

²¹Do you not know?
  Have you not heard?
  Have you not been told
  From the very first?
  Have you not discerned
  ᵈ⁻How the earth was founded?⁻ᵈ

²²It is He who is enthroned above the vault of the
      earth,
  So that its inhabitants seem as grasshoppers;
  Who spread out the skies like gauze,
  Stretched them out like a tent to dwell in.
²³He brings potentates to naught,
  Makes rulers of the earth as nothing.
²⁴Hardly are they planted,
  Hardly are they sown,
  Hardly has their stem
  Taken root in earth,
  When He blows upon them and they dry up,
  And the storm bears them off like straw.

²⁵To whom, then, can you liken Me,
  To whom can I be compared?
                          —says the Holy One.
²⁶Lift high your eyes and see:
  Who created these?
  He who sends out their host by count,
  Who calls them each by name:
  Because of His great might and vast power,
  Not one fails to appear.

²⁷Why do you say, O Jacob,
  Why declare, O Israel,
  "My way is hid from the LORD,
  My cause is ignored by my God"?
²⁸Do you not know?
  Have you not heard?
  The LORD is God from of old,
  Creator of the earth from end to end,
  He never grows faint or weary,
  Hs wisdom cannot be fathomed.
²⁹He gives strength to the weary,
  Fresh vigor to the spent.

ᵈ⁻ᵈ *Meaning of Heb uncertain*
ᵉ *Heb* mesukkan; *according to a Jewish tradition, preserved by Jerome, a kind of wood; a similar word denotes a kind of wood in Akkadian*

³⁰Youths may grow faint and weary,
  And young men stumble and fall;
³¹But they who trust in the Lord shall renew their
    strength
  As eagles grow new plumes:*
  They shall run and not grow weary,
  They shall march and not grow faint.

41

¹Stand silent before Me, coastlands,
  And let nations ᵃ⁻renew their strength.⁻ᵃ
  Let them approach to state their case;
  Let us come forward together for argument.
²Who has roused a victorᵇ from the East,
  Summoned him to His service?
  Has delivered up nations to him,
  And trodden sovereigns down?
  Has rendered theirᶜ swords like dust,
  Theirᶜ bows like wind-blown straw?
³He pursues them, he goes on unscathed;
  No shackleᵈ is placed on his feet.
⁴Who has wrought and achieved this?
  He who announced the generations from the
    start—
  I, the Lord, who was first
  And will be with the last as well.

⁵The coastlands look on in fear,
  The ends of earth tremble.

  They draw near and come;
⁶Each one helps the other,

  Saying to his fellow, "Take courage!"
⁷The woodworker encourages the smith;
  He who flattens with the hammer
  Encourages him who pounds the anvil.
  He says of the riveting, "It is good!"
  And he fixes it with nails,
  That it may not topple.

⁸But you, Israel, My servant,
  Jacob, whom I have chosen,
  Seed of Abraham My friend—
⁹You whom I led from the ends of the earth
  And called from its far corners,
  To whom I said: You are My servant;
  I chose you, I have not rejected you—
¹⁰Fear not, for I am with you,
  Be not frightened, for I am your God;
  I strengthen you and I help you,
  I uphold you with My gracious right hand.
¹¹Shamed and chagrined shall be
  All who contend with you;
  They who strive with you
  Shall become as naught and shall perish.
¹²You may seek, but shall not find
  Those who struggle with you;
  Less than nothing shall be
  The men who battle against you.
¹³For I the Lord am your God,
  I uphold your right hand,
  I say to you: Have no fear;
  I will be your help.

f   Alluding to a popular belief that eagles regain their youth
      when they molt; cf. Ps. 103.5

a-a Connection of Heb uncertain
b   Lit. "victory"
c   Heb "his"
d   'rḥ has this meaning in Old Aramaic

¹⁴Fear not, O worm Jacob,
  O ᵉ·men ofᵉ Israel:
  I will help you—declares the LORD—
  I your Redeemer, the Holy One of Israel.
¹⁵I will make of you a threshing-board,
  Sharp, new, with many spikes;
  You shall thresh mountains to dust,
  And make hills like chaff.
¹⁶You shall winnow them
  And the wind shall carry them off;
  The whirlwind shall scatter them.
  But you shall rejoice in the LORD,
  And glory in the Holy One of Israel.

¹⁷The poor and the needy
  Seek water,ᶠ and there is none;
  Their tongue is parched with thirst.
  I the LORD will respond to them.
  I, the God of Israel, will not forsake them.
¹⁸I will open up streams on the bare hills
  And fountains amid the valleys;
  I will turn the desert into ponds,
  The arid land into springs of water.
¹⁹I will plant cedars in the wilderness,
  Acacias and myrtles and oleasters;
  I will set cypresses in the desert,
  Box trees and elms as well—
²⁰That men may see and know,
  Consider and comprehend
  That the LORD's hand has done this,

That the Holy One of Israel has wrought it.

²¹Submit your case, says the LORD;
  Offer your pleas, says the King of Jacob.
²²Let them approachᵍ and tell us what will happen.
  Tell us what has occurred,ʰ
  And we will take note of it;
  Or announce to us what will occur,
  That we may know the outcome.
²³Foretell what is yet to happen,
  That we may know that you are gods!
  Do anything, good or bad,
  That we may be awed and see.ⁱ
²⁴Why, you are less than nothing,
  Your effect is less than nullity;
  One who chooses you is an abominaton.

²⁵I have roused him from the north, and he has
    come;
  From the sunrise, one who invokes My name.
  He has trampled rulers like mud,
  Like a potter treading clay.
²⁶Who foretold this from the start, that we may
    note it;
  From aforetime, that we might say, "He is
    right"?
  Not one foretold, not one announced;
  No one has heard your utterance!
²⁷ʲ·The things once predicted to Zion—
  Behold, here they are!·ʲ
  And again I send a herald to Jerusalem.
²⁸But I look and there is not a man,
  Of these, there is none who can predict
  Or can respond when I question him.
²⁹See, they are all nothingness,
  Their works are nullity,
  Their statues are naught and nil.

e-e *Emendation yields "maggot"*
f *I.e. on the homeward march through the desert*
g *Taking* yaggishu *intransitively; cf.* hiqriv, *Exod. 14.10*
h *I.e. former prophecies by your gods which have been ful-*
    filled
i *Change of vocalization yields "fear"; cf. v. 10*
j-j *Meaning of Heb uncertain*

42

¹This is My servant, whom I uphold,
  My chosen one, in whom I delight.
  I have put My spirit upon him,
  He shall teach the true way to the nations.
²He shall not cry out or shout aloud,
  Or make his voice heard in the streets.
³ᵃ⁻He shall not break even a bruised reed,
  Or snuff out even a dim wick.⁻ᵃ
  He shall bring forth the true way.
⁴He shall not grow dim or be bruised
  Till he has established the true way on earth;
  And the coastlands shall await his teaching.

⁵Thus said God the Lord,
  Who created the heavens and stretched them out,
  Who spread out the earth and what it brings
    forth,
  Who gave breath to the people upon it
  And life to those who walk thereon:
⁶I the Lord, in My grace, have summoned you,
  And I have grasped you by the hand.
  I created you, and appointed you
  A ᵇ⁻covenant-people,⁻ᵇ ᶜ⁻a light of nations—⁻ᶜ
⁷ᵈ⁻Opening eyes deprived of light,⁻ᵈ
  Rescuing prisoners from confinement,
  From the dungeon those who sit in darkness.
⁸I am the Lord, that is My name;
  I will not yield My glory to another,
  Nor My renown to idols.
⁹See, the things once predicted have come,
  And now I foretell new things,
  Announce to you ere they sprout up.

¹⁰Sing to the Lord a new song,
  His praise from the ends of the earth—
  ᵉ⁻You who sail the sea and you creatures in it,
  You coastlands⁻ᵉ and their inhabitants!
¹¹Let the desert and its towns cry aloud,
  The villages where Kedar dwells;
  Let Sela's inhabitants shout,
  Call out from the peaks of the mountains.
¹²Let them do honor to the Lord,
  And tell His glory in the coastlands.

¹³The Lord goes forth like a warrior,
  Like a fighter He whips up His rage.
  He yells, He roars aloud,
  He charges upon His enemies.
¹⁴"I have kept silent ᶠ⁻far too long,⁻ᶠ
  Kept still and restrained Myself;
  Now I will scream like a woman in labor,
  I will pant and I will gasp.
¹⁵Hills and heights will I scorch,
  Cause all their green to wither;
  I will turn rivers into isles,ᵍ
  And dry the marshes up.
¹⁶I will lead the blind
  By a road they did not know,
  And I will make them walk
  By paths they never knew.
  I will turn darkness before them to light,
  Rough places into level ground.

a-a Or "A bruised reed, he shall not be broken;
        A dim wick, he shall not be snuffed out"
b-b Lit. "covenant of a people"; exact force of Heb uncertain
c-c See 49.6 and note
d-d An idiom meaning "freeing the imprisoned"; cf. Isa. 61.2
e-e Emendation yields "Let the sea roar and its creatures,
        The coastlands . . ."
f-f Lit. "from of old"
g Emendation yields "desert"

These are the promises—
I will keep them without fail.
¹⁷Driven back and utterly shamed
Shall be those who trust in an image,
Those who say to idols,
'You are our gods!' "

¹⁸Listen, you who are deaf;
You blind ones, look up and see!
¹⁹Who is so blind as My servant,
So deaf as the messenger I send?
Who is so blind as the chosen[h] one,
So blind as the servant of the LORD?
²⁰Seeing many things, [i]he gives[i] no heed;
With ears open, he hears nothing.
²¹[j]It pleases the LORD, for His vindication,
That [His servant] magnify and glorify Teach-
ing.

²²Yet it is a people plundered and despoiled:
All of them are trapped in holes,
Imprisoned in dungeons.
They are given over to plunder, with none to
rescue them;
To despoilment, with none to say "Give back!"
²³If only you would listen to this,
Attend and give heed from now on!
²⁴Who was it gave Jacob over to despoilment
And Israel to plunderers?
Surely, the LORD against whom they[k] sinned
In whose ways they would not walk
And whose Teaching they would not obey.

h   Meaning of Heb uncertain
i-i   Heb "you give"
j   Meaning of verse uncertain
k   Heb "we"

²⁵So He poured out wrath upon them,
His anger and the fury of war.
It blazed upon them all about, but they heeded
not;
It burned among them, but they gave it no
thought.

43

¹But now, thus said the LORD—
Who created you, O Jacob,
Who formed you, O Israel:
Fear not, for I will redeem you;
I have singled you out by name,
You are Mine.
²When you pass through water,
I will be with you;
Through streams,
They shall not overwhelm you.
When you walk through fire,
You shall not be scorched;
Through flame,
It shall not burn you.
³For I the LORD am your God,
The Holy One of Israel, your Savior.
I give Egypt as a ransom for you,
Ethiopia and Saba in exchange for you.
⁴Because you are precious to Me,
And honored, and I love you,
I give men in exchange for you
And peoples in your stead.

⁵Fear not, for I am with you:

I will bring your folk from the East,
Will gather you out of the West;
⁶I will say to the North, "Give back!"
And to the South, "Do not withhold!
Bring My sons from afar,
And My daughters from the end of the earth—
⁷All who are linked to My name,
Whom I have created,
Formed, and made for My glory—
⁸Setting free that people,
Blind though it has eyes
And deaf though it has ears."

⁹All the nations assemble as one,
The peoples gather.
Who among them declared this,
Foretold to us the things that have happened?
Let them produce their witnesses and be vindi-
cated,
That men, hearing them, may say, "It is true!"ᵃ
¹⁰You are My witnesses
—declares the LORD—
My servant, whom I have chosen.
To the end that youᵇ may take thought,
And believe in Me,
And understand that I am He:
Before Me no god was formed,
And after Me none shall exist.
¹¹I, I am the LORD;
Beside Me, none can grant triumph.
¹²I alone foretold the triumph
And I brought it to pass;
I announced it,
And no strange god was among you.
So you are My witnesses
—declares the LORD—

And I am God.
¹³Ever since day was, I am He;
None can deliver from My hand.
When I act, who can reverse it?

¹⁴Thus said the LORD,
Your Redeemer, the Holy One of Israel:
For your sake ᶜI send to Babylon;
I will bring down all [her] bars,
And the Chaldeans shall raise their voice in lamen-
tation.ᶜ
¹⁵I am the LORD, your Holy One.
The Creator of Israel, your King.

¹⁶Thus said the LORD,
Who made a road through the sea
And a path through mighty waters,
¹⁷Who destroyedᵈ chariots and horses,
And all the mighty host—
They lay down to rise no more,
They were extinguished, quenched like a wick:
¹⁸Do not recall what happened of old,
Or ponder what happened of yore!
¹⁹I am about to do something new;
Even now it shall come to pass,
Suddenly you shall perceive it:
I will make a road through the wilderness
And riversᵉ in the desert.
²⁰The wild beasts shall honor Me,
Jackals and ostriches,
For I provide water in the wilderness,

a   I.e. that the other nations' gods are real
b   Emendation yields "they"
c-c   Meaning of Heb uncertain
d   Ḥoṣi is here equivalent to Aramaic sheṣi
e   Ms. 1QIsᵃ reads "paths"; cf. v. 16

Rivers in the desert,
To give drink to My chosen people,
²¹The people I formed for Myself
That they might declare my praise.

²²But you have not worshiped Me, O Jacob,
That you should be weary of Me, O Israel.
²³You have not brought Me your sheep for burnt
offerings,
Nor honored Me with your sacrifices.
I have not burdened you with meal offerings,
Nor wearied you about frankincense.
²⁴You have not bought Me fragrant reed with
money,
Nor sated Me with the fat of your sacrifices.
Instead, you have burdened Me with your sins,
You have wearied Me with your iniquities.
²⁵It is I, I, who—for My own sake*ᶠ*—
Wipe your transgressions away
And remember your sins no more.
²⁶Help me remember!
Let us join in argument,
Tell your version,
That you may be vindicated.
²⁷Your earliest ancestor sinned,
And your spokesmen transgressed against Me.
²⁸So I profaned *ᵍ*the holy princes;*ᵍ*
I abandoned Jacob to proscription*ʰ*
And Israel to mockery.

f   *I.e. in order to put an end to the profanation of My Holy*
Name; cf. 48.9-11
g-g *Emendation yields "My Holy Name"; see preceding note*
h   *Emendation yields "insult"*

a   *A name for Israel; see note on Nu. 23.10; cf. Deut. 32.15;*
33.5, 26
b   *Lit. "in among"*
c   *It was customary to mark a slave with the owner's name*
d   *Meaning of verse uncertain*

44

¹But hear, now, O Jacob My servant,
Israel whom I have chosen!
²Thus said the LORD, your Maker,
Your Creator who has helped you since birth:
Fear not, My servant Jacob,
Jeshurun*ᵃ* whom I have chosen,
³Even as I pour water on thirsty soil,
And rain upon dry ground,
So will I pour My spirit on your offspring,
My blessing upon your posterity.
⁴And they shall sprout like*ᵇ* grass,
Like willows by watercourses.
⁵One shall say, "I am the LORD's,"
Another shall use the name of "Jacob,"
Another shall mark his arm "of the LORD"*ᶜ*
And adopt the name of "Israel."

⁶Thus said the LORD, the King of Israel,
Their Redeemer, the LORD of Hosts:
I am the first and I am the last,
And there is no god but Me.
⁷*ᵈ*Who like Me can announce,
Can foretell it—and match Me thereby?
Even as I told the future to an ancient people,
So let him foretell coming events to them.
⁸Do not be frightened, do not be shaken!
Have I not from of old predicted to you?
I foretold, and you are My witnesses.
Is there any god, then, but Me?
"There is no other rock; I know none!"

⁹The makers of idols
All work to no purpose;

And the things they treasure
Can do no good,
As they themselves can testify.
They neither look nor think,
And so they shall be shamed.
¹⁰Who would fashion a god
Or cast a statue
That can do no good?
¹¹Lo, all its adherents shall be shamed;
They are craftsmen, are merely human.
Let them all assemble and stand up!
They shall be cowed, and they shall be shamed.

¹²ᵉThe craftsman in iron, with his tools,
Works itᶠ over charcoal
And fashions it by hammering,
Working with the strength of his arm.
Should he go hungry, his strength would ebb;
Should he drink no water, he would grow faint.

¹³The craftman in wood measures with a line
And marks out a shape with a stylus;
He forms it with scraping tools,
Marking it out with a compass.
He gives it a human form,
The beauty of a man, to dwell in a shrine.
¹⁴For his use he cuts down cedars;
He chooses plane trees and oaks.
He sets aside trees of the forest;
Or plants firs, and the rain makes them grow.
¹⁵All this serves man for fuel:
He takes some to warm himself,
And he builds a fire and bakes bread.
He also makes a god of it and worships it,
Fashions an idol and bows down to it!
¹⁶Part of it he burns in a fire:

On that part he roastsᵍ meat,
He eatsᵍ the roast and is sated;
He also warms himself and cries, "Ah,
I am warm! I can feelʰ the heat!"
¹⁷Of the rest he makes a god—his own carving!
He bows down to it, worships it;
He prays to it and cries,
"Save me, for you are my god!"

¹⁸They have no wit or judgment:
Their eyes are besmeared, and they see not;
Their minds, and they cannot think.
¹⁹They do not give thought,
They lack the wit and judgment to say:
"Part of it I burned in a fire;
I also baked bread on the coals,
I roasted meat and ate it—
Should I make the rest an abhorrence?
Should I bow to a block of wood?"
²⁰He pursues ashes!ⁱ
A deluded mind has led him astray,
And he cannot save himself;
He never says to himself,
"The thing in my hand is a fraud!"

²¹Remember these things, O Jacob
For you, O Israel, are My servant:
I fashioned you, you are My servant—
O Israel, never forget Me.ʲ
²²I wipe away your sins like a cloud,
Your transgressions like mist—

e   *The meaning of parts of vv. 12-13 is uncertain*
f   *I.e. the image he is making*
g   *Transposing the Heb verbs for clarity*
h   *Lit. "see"*
i   *Lit. "He shepherds ashes"*
j   *Emendation yields "them"*

Come back to Me, for I redeem you.

23Shout, O heavens, for the Lord has acted;
  Shout aloud, O depths of the earth!
  Shout for joy, O mountains,
  O forests with all your trees!
  For the Lord has redeemed Jacob,
  Has glorified Himself through Israel.

24Thus said the Lord, your Redeemer,
  Who formed you in the womb:
  It is I, the Lord, who made everything,
  Who alone stretched out the heavens
  And unaided*k* spread out the earth;
25Who annul the omens of diviners,
  And make fools of the augurs;
  Who turn sages back
  And make nonsense of their knowledge;
26But confirm the word of My*l* servant
  And fulfill the prediction of My*l* messengers.
  It is I who say of Jerusalem, "It shall be in-
    habited,"
  And of the towns of Judah, "They shall be re-
    built;
  And I will restore their ruined places."
27[I,] who said to the deep, "Be dry;
  I will dry up your floods,"
28Am the same who says of Cyrus, "He is My
    shepherd*m*;
  He shall fulfill all My purposes!

---

k *Lit. "with none beside me," or (following many Heb mss.,*
    Kethib, and ancient versions) "who was with me?"
l *Heb "His"*
m *I.e. the king whom I have designated*

a-a *Heb "I have"*
b-b *I.e. I made them helpless; one who wished to move freely*
    belted his garment around the waist; cf. "engird" v. 5
c-c *Meaning of Heb uncertain*

He shall say of Jerusalem, 'She shall be rebuilt,'
And to the Temple: 'You shall be founded
again.' "

45

1Thus said the Lord to Cyrus, His anointed one—
  Whose right hand *a*-He has-*a* grasped,
  Treading down nations before him,
  b-Ungirding the loins of kings,-*b*
  Opening doors before him
  And letting no gate stay shut:
2I will march before you
  And level *c*-the hills that loom up;-*c*
  I will shatter doors of bronze
  And cut down iron bars.
3I will give you treasures concealed in the dark
  And secret hoards—
  So that you may know that I am the Lord,
  The God of Israel, who call you by name.
4For the sake of My servant Jacob,
  Israel My chosen one,
  I call you by name,
  I hail you by title, though you have not known
    Me.
5I am the Lord and there is none else;
  Beside Me, there is no god.
  I engird you, though you have not known Me,
6So that they may know, from east to west,
  That there is none but Me,
  I am the Lord and there is none else,
7I form light and create darkness,
  I make weal and create woe—
  I the Lord do all these things.

⁸Pour down, O skies, from above!
Let the heavens rain down victory!
Let the earth open up and triumph sprout,
Yes, let vindication spring up:
I the LORD have created it.

⁹Shame on him who argues with his Maker,
Though naught but a potsherd of earth!
Shall the clay say to the potter, "What are you
doing?
ᵈ⁻Your work has no handles"?⁻ᵈ
¹⁰Shame on him who asks his father, "What are
you begetting?"
Or a woman, "What are you bearing?"

¹¹Thus said the LORD,
Israel's Holy One and Maker:
ᵉ⁻Will you question Me⁻ᵉ on the destiny of My
children,
Will you instruct Me about the work of My
hands?
¹²It was I who made the earth
And created man upon it;
My own hands stretched out the heavens,
And I marshalled all their host.
¹³It was I who roused himᶠ for victory
And who level all roads for him.
He shall rebuild My city
And let My exiled people go
Without price and without payment—
Said the LORD of Hosts.

¹⁴Thus said the LORD:
Egypt's wealth and Nubia's gains
And men of Seba, ᵍlong of limb,⁻ᵍ
Shall pass over to you and be yours,
Pass over and follow you in fetters,

Bow low to you
And reverently address you:
"Only among you is God,
There is no other god at all!
¹⁵You are indeed a God who concealed Himself,
O God of Israel, who bring victory!
¹⁶Those who fabricate idols,
Shamed are they and disgraced,
All of them, to a man.
¹⁷But Israel has won through the LORD
Triumph everlasting.
You shall not be shamed or disgraced
In all the ages to come!"

¹⁸For thus said the LORD,
The Creator of heaven who alone is God,
Who formed the earth and made it,
Who alone established it—
He did not create it a waste,
But formed it for habitation:
I am the LORD, and there is none else.
¹⁹I did not speak in secret,
At a site in a land of darkness;
I did not say to the stock of Jacob,
"Seek Me out in a wasteland"—
I the LORD, who foretell reliably,
Who announce what is true.

²⁰Come, gather together,
Draw nigh, you remnants of the nations!
No foreknowledge had they who carry their
wooden images

d-d *Emendation yields "To its Maker, 'You have no hands'?"*
e-e *Heb imperative*
f *I.e. Cyrus*
g-g *Emendation yields "bearing tribute." For "tribute" cf. Ezra*
4.20; 6.8; Neh. 5.4

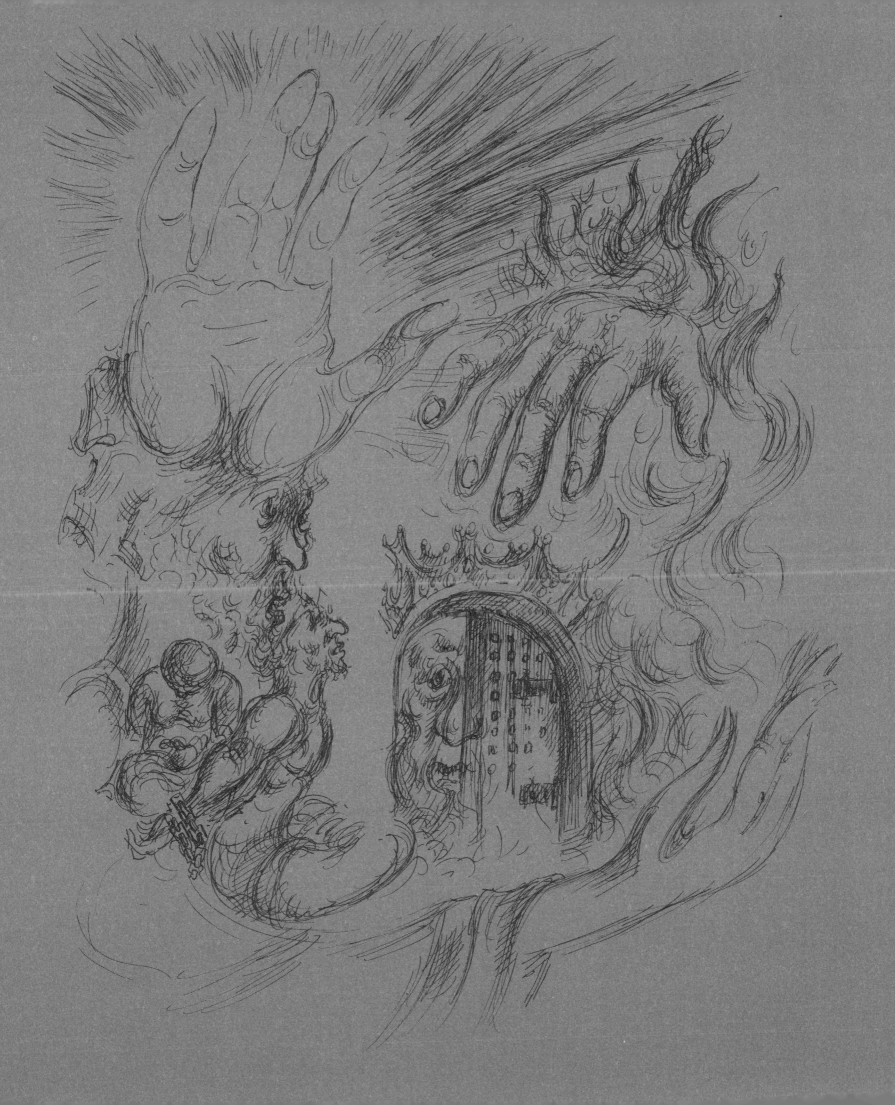

And pray to a god who cannot give success.
21Speak up, compare testimony—
Let them even take counsel together!
Who announced this aforetime,
Foretold it of old?
Was it not I the LORD?
Then there is no god beside Me,
No God exists beside Me
Who foretells truly and grants success.
22Turn to Me and gain success,
All the ends of earth!
For I am God, and there is none else.
23By Myself have I sworn,
From My mouth has issued truth,
A word that shall not turn back:
To Me every knee shall bend,
Every tongue swear loyalty.
24They shall say: h-"Only through the LORD
Can I find victory and might."-h
When one i-trusts in-i Him,
All his adversaries are put to shame.
25It is through the LORD that all the offspring of
Israel
Have vindication and glory."

46

1Bela is bowed, Neboa is cowering,
Their images are a burden for beasts and cattle;

h-h Emendation yields "Only in the LORD
Are there victory and might for man"
i-i Lit. "come to"; for this idiom cf. Ps. 65.3; Job 6.20

a A Babylonian deity
b Emendation yields "they"
c Emendation yields "him who carried [them]"; cf. Targum
d Lit. "beam (of the balance)"
e-e Meaning of Heb uncertain

The things youb would carry [in procession]
Are now piled as a burden
On tired [beasts].
2They cowered, they bowed as well,
They could not rescue the burden,c
And they themselves went into captivity.

3Listen to Me, O House of Jacob,
All that are left of the House of Israel,
Who have been carried since birth,
Supported since leaving the womb—
4Till you grow old, I will still be the same;
When you turn gray, it is I who will carry;
I was the Maker, and I will be the Bearer;
And I will carry and rescue [you].

5To whom can you compare Me
Or declare Me similar?
To whom can you liken Me,
So that we seem comparable?
6Those who squander gold from the purse
And weigh out silver on the balance,d
They hire a metal worker to make it into a god,
To which they bow down and prostrate them-
selves.
7They must carry it on their backs and transport
it;
When they put it down, it stands,
It does not budge from its place.
If they cry out to it, it does not answer;
It cannot save them from their distress.
8Keep this in mind, and e-stand firm!-e
Take this to heart, you sinners!
9Bear in mind what happened of old;
For I am God, and there is none else,
I am divine, and there is none like Me.

¹⁰I foretell the end from the beginning,
And from the start, things that had not occurred.
I say: My plan shall be fulfilled;
I will do all I have purposed.
¹¹I summoned that swooping bird from the East^f;
From a distant land, the man for My purpose.
I have spoken, so I will bring it to pass;
I have designed it, so I will complete it.
¹²Listen to Me, ^{g-}you stubborn of heart,^{-g}
Who are far from victory:
¹³I am bringing My victory close;
It shall not be far,
And My triumph shall not be delayed.
I will grant triumph in Zion,
My glory to Israel.

47

¹Get down, sit in the dust,
Fair Maiden Babylon;
Sit, dethroned, on the ground,
O Fair Chaldea;
Nevermore shall they call you
The tender and dainty one.
²Grasp the handmill and grind meal.
Remove your veil,
Strip off your train, bare your leg,
Wade through the rivers.
³Your nakedness shall be uncovered,
And your shame shall be exposed.
I will take vengeance,
^{a-}And let no man intercede.
⁴Our Redeemer—Lord of Hosts is His name—

Is the Holy One of Israel.^{-a}
⁵Sit silent; retire into darkness,
O Fair Chaldea;
Nevermore shall they call you
Mistress of Kingdoms.

⁶I was angry at My people,
I defiled My heritage;
I put them into your hands,
But you showed them no mercy.
Even upon the aged you made
Your yoke exceedingly heavy.
⁷You thought, "I shall always be
The mistress still."
You did not take these things to heart,
You gave no thought to the end of it.

⁸And now hear this, O pampered one—
Who dwell in security,
Who think to yourself,
"I am, and there is none but me;
I shall not become a widow
Or know loss of children"—
⁹These two things shall come upon you,
Suddenly, in one day:
Loss of children and widowhood
Shall come upon you in full measure,
Despite your many enchantments
And all your countless spells.
¹⁰You were secure in your wickedness;
You thought, "No one can see me."

f   *I.e. Cyrus; cf. 41.2-3*
g-g *Septuagint reads, "who have lost heart"*

a-a *Meaning of Heb uncertain; emendation yields*
        "And not be appeased,
        Says our Redeemer, whose name is Lord *of Hosts,*
        The Holy One of Israel"

It was your skill and your science
That led you astray.
And you thought to yourself,
"I am, and there is none but me."
¹¹Evil is coming upon you
Which you will not know how to ᵇ‐charm away‐ᵇ;
Disaster is falling upon you
Which you will not be able to appease;
Coming upon you suddenly
Is ruin of which you know nothing.
¹²Stand up, with your spells and your many en-
    chantments
On which you labored since youth!
Perhaps you'll be able to profit,
Perhaps you ᶜ‐will find strength.‐ᶜ
¹³You are helpless, despite all your art.
Let them stand up and help you now,
The scannersᵈ of heaven, the star-gazers,
Who announce, month by month,
Whatever will come upon you.
¹⁴See, they are become like straw,
Fire consumes them;
They cannot save themselves
From the power of the flame;
This is no coal for warming oneself,
No fire to sit by!
¹⁵This is what they have profited you—
The traders you dealt with since youth—
Each has wandered off his own way,
There is none to save you.

b-b *Meaning of Heb uncertain; emendation yields "bribe"*
c-c *Taking ʿaraṣ as a variant of ʿaṣar; cf. II Chr. 20.37*
d   *Meaning of Heb uncertain*

a   *Emendation yields "loins"*
b   *Heb "they"*
c-c *Emendation yields "the holy people"*
d-d *Meaning of Heb uncertain*

48

¹Listen to this, O House of Jacob,
Who call yourselves Israel
And have issued from the watersᵃ of Judah,
Who swear by the name of the LORD
And invoke the God of Israel—
Though not in truth and sincerity—
²For youᵇ are called after ᶜ‐the Holy City‐ᶜ
And youᵇ do lean on the God of Israel,
Whose name is LORD of Hosts:

³Long ago, I foretold things that happened,
From My mouth they issued, and I announced
    them;
Suddenly I acted, and they came to pass.
⁴Because I know how stubborn you are
(Your neck is like an iron sinew
And your forehead bronze),
⁵Therefore I told you long beforehand,
Announced things to you ere they happened—
That you might not say, "My idol caused them,
My carved and molten images ordained them."
⁶You have ᵈ‐heard all this; look, must you not
    acknowledge it?‐ᵈ
As of now, I announce to you new things,
Well-guarded secrets you did not know.
⁷Only now are they created, and not of old;
ᵈ‐Before today‐ᵈ you had not heard them;
You cannot say, "I knew them already."
⁸You had never heard, you had never known,
Your ears were not opened of old.

Though I know that you are treacherous,
That you were called a rebel from birth,

⁹For the sake of My name I control My wrath;
　To my own glory, ᵈ·I am patient·ᵈ with you,
　And I will not destroy you.
¹⁰See, I refine you, but not as silver;
　I test you in the furnace of affliction.
¹¹For My sake, My own sake, do I act—
　Lest [My name]ᵉ be dishonored!
　I will not give My glory to another.

¹²Listen to Me, O Jacob,
　Israel, whom I have called:
　I am He—I am the first,
　And I am the last as well.
¹³My own hand founded the earth,
　My right hand spread out the skies.

　I call unto them, let them stand up.
¹⁴Assemble, all of you, and listen!
　Who among youᶠ foretold these things:
　ᵈ·"He whom the Lᴏʀᴅ loves
　Shall work His will against Babylon,
　And, with his might, against Chaldeans"?·ᵈ
¹⁵I, I predicted, and I called him;
　I have brought him and he shall succeed in his
　　mission.
¹⁶Draw near to Me and hear this:
　From the beginning, I did not speak in secret;
　From the time anything existed, I was there.ᵍ

　"And now the Lord God has sent me, ʰ·endowed
　　with His spirit."·ʰ

¹⁷Thus said the Lᴏʀᴅ your Redeemer.
　The Holy One of Israel:
　I the Lᴏʀᴅ am your God,
　Instructing you for your own benefit.

　Guiding you in the way you should go.
¹⁸If only you would heed My commands!
　Then your prosperity would be like a river,
　Your triumph like the waves of the sea.
¹⁹Your offspring would be as many as the sand,
　Their issue as many as its grains.ᵈ
　Their name would never be cut off
　Or obliterated from before Me.

²⁰Go forth from Babylon,
　Flee from Chaldea!
　Declare this with loud shouting,
　Announce this,
　Bring out the word to the ends of the earth!
²¹Say: "The Lᴏʀᴅ has redeemed
　His servant Jacob!"
　They have known no thirst,
　Though He led them through parched places;
　He made water flow for them from the rock;
　He cleaved the rock and water gushed forth.

²²There is no safety—said the Lᴏʀᴅ—for the wicked.

49

¹Listen, O coastlands to me,
　And give heed, O nations afar:
　The Lᴏʀᴅ appointed me before I was born,
　He named me while I was in my mother's womb.

d-d　*Meaning of Heb uncertain*
e　　*These words are supplied in some ancient versions*
f　　*Heb "them"*
g　　*I.e. I sent prophets; cf. 45.19*
h-h　*Lit. "and His spirit"*

²He made my mouth like a sharpened blade,
  He hid me in the shadow of His hand,
  And He made me like a polished arrow;
  He concealed me in His quiver.
³And He said to me, "You are My servant,
  Israel in whom I glory."
⁴I thought, "I have labored in vain,
  I have spent my strength for empty breath."
  But my case rested with the Lord,
  My recompense was in the hands of my God.
⁵And now the Lord has resolved—
  He who formed me in the womb to be His ser-
    vant—
  To bring back Jacob to Himself,
  That Israel may be restored to Him.
  And I have been honored in the sight of the Lord,
  My God has been my strength.
⁶For He has said:
  "It is too little that you should be My servant
  In that I raise up the tribes of Jacob
  And restore the survivors of Israel:
  I will also make you a light^a of nations,
  That My salvation may reach the ends of the
    earth."

⁷Thus said the Lord,
  The Redeemer of Israel, his Holy One,
  ^b·To the despised one,
  To the abhorred nations,·^b
  To the slave of rulers:
  Kings shall see and stand up;

Nobles, and they shall prostrate themselves—
  To the honor of the Lord, who is faithful,
  To the Holy One of Israel who chose you.

⁸Thus said the Lord:
  In an hour of favor I answer you,
  And on a day of salvation I help you—
  I created you and appointed you ^c·a covenant
    people—·^c
  Restoring the land,
  Allotting anew the desolate holdings,
⁹Saying to the prisoners, "Go free,"
  To those who are in darkness, "Show yourselves."
  They shall pasture along the roads,
  On every bare height shall be their pasture.
¹⁰They shall not hunger or thirst,
  Hot wind and sun shall not strike them;
  For He who loves them will lead them,
  He will guide them to springs of water.
¹¹I will make all My mountains a road,
  And My highways shall be built up.
¹²Look! These are coming from afar,
  These from the north and the west,
  And these from the land of Sinim.^d
¹³Shout, O heavens, and rejoice, O earth!
  Break into shouting, O hills!
  For the Lord has comforted His people,
  And has taken back His afflicted ones in love.

¹⁴Zion says,
  "The Lord has forsaken me,
  My Lord has forgotten me."
¹⁵Can a woman forget her baby,
  Or disown the child of her womb?
  Though she might forget,
  I never could forget you.

a   I.e. the agent of good fortune; cf. 42.1-4; 51.4-5
b-b Meaning of Heb uncertain. Emendation yields
        "Whose being is despised,
        Whose body is detested"; cf. 51.23
c-c See note at 42.6
d   Manuscript 1QIs^a reads "the Syenians"; cf. Ezek. 30.6

16See, I have engraved you
  On the palms of My hands,
  Your walls are ever before Me.
17Swiftly your children are coming;
  Those who ravaged and ruined you shall leave
    you.
18Look up all around you and see:
  They are all assembled, are come to you!
  As I live—declares the Lord—
  You shall don them all like jewels,
  Deck yourself with them like a bride.
19As for your ruins and desolate places
  And your land laid waste—
  You shall soon be crowded with settlers,
  While destroyers stay far from you.
20The children e-you thought you had lost-e
  Shall yet say in your hearing,
  "The place is too crowded for me;
  Make room for me to settle."
21And you will say to yourself,
  "Who bore these for me
  When I was bereaved and barren,
  Exiled and disdained—f
  By whom, then were these reared?
  I was left all alone—
  And where have these been?"

22Thus said the Lord God:
  I will raise My hand to nations
  And lift up My ensign to peoples;
  And they shall bring your sons in their bosoms,
  And carry your daughters on their shoulders.
23Kings shall tend your children,
  Their queens shall serve you as nurses.
  They shall bow to you, face to the ground,
  And lick the dust of your feet.

And you shall know that I am the Lord—
  Those who trust in Me shall not be shamed.

24Can spoil be taken from a warrior,
  Or captives retrieved from a victor?
25Yet thus said the Lord:
  Captives shall be taken from a warrior
  And spoil shall be retrieved from a tyrant;
  For I will contend with your adversaries,
  And I will deliver your children.
26I will make your oppressors eat their own flesh,
  They shall be drunk with their own blood as
    with wine.
  And all mankind shall know
  That I the Lord am your Savior,
  The Mighty One of Jacob, your Redeemer.

50

1Thus said the Lord:
aWhere is the bill of divorce
  Of your mother whom I dismissed?
  And which of My creditors was it
  To whom I sold you off?
  You were only sold off for your sins,
  And your mother dismissed for your crimes.
2Why, when I came, was no one there,
  Why, when I called, would none respond?
  Is my arm, then, too short to rescue,

e-e Lit. "of your bereavement"
f   Meaning of Heb uncertain

a   The mother (the country) has not been formally divorced,
    nor the children (the inhabitants) sold because of poverty.
    Therefore there is no obstacle to their restoration

Have I not the power to save?
With a mere rebuke I dry up the sea,
And turn rivers into desert.
Their fish stink from lack of water;
They lie dead *b·*of thirst.*·b*
³I clothe the skies in blackness
And make their raiment sackcloth.

⁴*c·*The Lord GOD gave me a skilled tongue,
To know how to speak timely words to the
weary.*·c*
Morning by morning, He rouses,
He rouses my ear
To give heed like disciples.
⁵The Lord GOD opened my ears,
And I did not disobey,
I did not run away.
⁶I offered my back to the floggers,
And my cheeks to those who tore out my hair.
I did not hide my face
From insult and spittle.
⁷But the Lord GOD will help me—
Therefore I feel no disgrace;
Therefore I have set my face like flint,
And I know I shall not be shamed.
⁸My Vindicator is at hand—
Who dare contend with me?
Let us stand up together!*d*
Who would be my opponent?
Let him approach me!
⁹Lo, the Lord GOD will help me—
Who can get a verdict against me?

b-b *Change of vocalization yields "on the parched ground";*
cf. 44.3
c-c *Meaning of Heb uncertain*
d *I.e. as opponents in court; cf. Nu. 35.12*
e-e *Emendation yields "lighters of"*

They shall all wear out like a garment,
The moth shall consume them.

¹⁰Who among you reveres the LORD
And heeds the voice of His servant?—
Though he walk in darkness
And have no light,
Let him trust in the name of the LORD
And rely upon his God.
¹¹But you are all kindlers of fire,
*e·*Girding on*·e* firebrands.
Walk by the blaze of your fire,
By the brands that you have lit!
This has come to you from My hand:
*c·*You shall lie down in pain.*·c*

51

¹Listen to Me, you who pursue justice,
You who seek the LORD:
Look to the rock you were hewn from,
To the quarry you were dug from.
²Look back to Abraham your father
And to Sarah who brought you forth.
For he was only one when I called him,
But I blessed him and made him many.

³Truly the LORD has comforted Zion,
Comforted all her ruins;
He has made her wilderness like Eden,
Her desert like the Garden of the LORD.
Gladness and joy shall abide there,
Thanksgiving and the sound of music.

⁴Hearken to Me, ᵃ⁻My people,⁻ᵃ
And give ear to Me, O ᵃ⁻My nation,⁻ᵃ
For teaching shall go forthᵇ from Me,
My way for the light of peoples.
In a moment I will bring it:
⁵The triumph I grant is near,
The success I give has gone forth.
My arms shall ᶜ⁻provide for⁻ᶜ the peoples;
The coastlands shall trust in Me,
They shall look to My arm.

⁶Raise your eyes to the heavens,
And look upon the earth beneath:
Though the heavens should melt away like smoke,
And the earth wear out like a garment,
And its inhabitants die out ᵈ⁻as well,⁻ᵈ
My victory shall stand forever,
My triumph shall remain unbroken.

⁷Listen to Me, you who care for the right,
O people who lay My instruction to heart!
Fear not the insults of men,
And be not dismayed at their jeers;
⁸For the moth shall eat them up like a garment,
The wormᵉ shall eat them up like wool.
But My triumph shall endure forever,
My salvation through all the ages.

⁹Awake, awake, clothe yourself with splendor.
O arm of the LORD!
Awake as in days of old,
As in former ages!
It was you that hacked Rahabᶠ in pieces,
That pierced the Dragon.ᶠ
¹⁰It was You that dried up the Sea,
The waters of the great deep;

That made the abysses of the Sea
A road the redeemed might walk.
¹¹So let the ransomed of the LORD return,
And come with shouting to Zion,
Crowned with joy everlasting.
Let them attain joy and gladness,
While sorrow and sighing flee.

¹²I, I am He who comforts you!
What ails you that you fear
Man who must die,
Mortals who fare like grass?
¹³You have forgotten the LORD your Maker,
Who stretched out the skies and made firm the
   earth!
And you live all day in constant dread
Because of the rage of an oppressor
Who is aiming to cut [you] down.
Yet of what account is the rage of an oppressor?
¹⁴ᵍQuickly the crouching one is freed;
He is not cut down and slain,
And he shall not want for food.
¹⁵For I the LORD your God—
Who stir up the sea into roaring waves,
Whose name is LORD of Hosts—
¹⁶ʰ⁻Have put My words in your mouth
And sheltered you with My hand;⁻ʰ

a-a *Several mss. read "O people . . . O nations"; cf. end of this
      verse and verse 5*
b   *I.e. through My servant Israel; cf. 42.1-5: 49.6*
c-c *Lit. "judge"*
d-d *Emendation yields "like gnats"*
e   *Heb sas, another word for "moth"*
f   *Names of primeval monsters*
g   *Meaning of verse uncertain. Emendation yields (cf. Jer.
      11.9b; Job 14.7-9)*
        "Quickly the tree buds anew;
          It does not die though cut down,
          And its sap does not fail"
h   *I.e. I have chosen you to be a prophet-nation; cf. 49.2; 59.21*

I, who planted*i* the skies and made firm the earth,
Have said to Zion: You are My people!
¹⁷Rouse, rouse yourself!
Arise, O Jerusalem,
You who from the LORD's hand
Have drunk the cup of His wrath,
You who have drained to the dregs
The bowl, the cup of reeling!
¹⁸She has none to guide her
Of all the sons she bore;
None takes her by the hand,
Of all the sons she reared.*j*
¹⁹These two things have befallen you:
Wrack and ruin—who can console you?
Famine and sword—*k⁻*how shall I*⁻k* comfort you?
²⁰Your sons lie in a swoon
At the corner of every street—
Like an antelope caught in a net—
Drunk with the wrath of the LORD,
With the rebuke of your God.
²¹Therefore,
Listen to this, unhappy one,
Who are drunk, but not with wine!
²²Thus said the LORD, your Lord,
Your God who champions His people:
Herewith I take from your hand
The cup of reeling,*l*
The bowl, the cup of My wrath;
You shall never drink it again.

---

i   *Emendation yields "stretched out"; cf. Syriac version and v. 13*

j   *To guide a drunken parent home was a recognized filial duty in ancient Canaan and Egypt*

k-k *Several ancient versions render "who can"*

l   *A figure of speech for a dire fate; cf. Jer. 25.15 ff.*

a   *Whereas the Israelites themselves sought hospitality in Egypt, Assyria (i.e. the Chaldean Empire) has exiled them by force*

²³I will put it in the hands of your tormentors,
Who have commanded you,
"Get down, that we may walk over you"—
So that you made your back like the ground,
Like a street for passers-by.

52

¹Awake, awake, O Zion!
Clothe yourself in splendor;
Put on your robes of majesty,
Jerusalem, holy city!
For the uncircumcised and the unclean
Shall never enter you again.
²Arise, shake off the dust,
Sit [on your throne], Jerusalem!
Loose the bonds from your neck
O captive one, Fair Zion!

³For thus said the LORD:
You were sold for no price,
And shall be redeemed without money.
⁴For thus said the Lord GOD:
Of old, My people went down
To Egypt to sojourn there;
But Assyria has robbed them,
Giving nothing in return.*a*
⁵What therefore do I gain here?
        —declares the LORD—
For My people has been carried off for nothing,
Their mockers howl
        —declares the LORD—
And constantly, unceasingly,

My name is reviled.
⁶Assuredly, My people shall learn My name,
Assuredly [they shall learn] on that day
That I, the one who promised,
Am now at hand.

⁷How welcome on the mountain
Are the footsteps of the herald
Announcing happiness,
Heralding good fortune,
Announcing victory,
Telling Zion, "Your God is King!"
⁸Hark!
Your watchmen raise their voices,
As one they shout for joy;
For every eye shall behold
The Lord's return to Zion.
⁹Raise a shout together,
O ruins of Jerusalem!
For the Lord will comfort His people,
Will redeem Jerusalem.
¹⁰The Lord will bare His holy arm
In the sight of all the nations,
And the very ends of earth shall see
The victory of our God.

¹¹Turn, turn away, touch naught unclean
As you depart from there;
Keep pure, as you go forth from there,
You who bear the vessels of the Lord!ᵇ
¹²For you will not depart in haste,
Nor will you leave in flight;
For the Lord is marching before you,
The God of Israel is your rear guard.

¹³Indeed, My servant shall prosper,

Be exalted and raised to great heights.
¹⁴Just as the many were appalled at himᵉ—
So marred was his appearance, unlike that of man,
His form, beyond human semblance—
¹⁵Just so he shall startleᵈ many nations.
Kings shall be silenced because of him,
For they shall see what has not been told them,
Shall behold what they never have heard.

53

¹Who can believe what we have heard?
Upon whom has ᵃ⁻the arm of the Lord⁻ᵃ been
    revealed?
²For he has grown, by His favor, like a sapling,
Like a root out of arid ground.
He had no form or beauty, that we should look
    at him:
No charm, that we should find him pleasing.
³He was despised, ᵇ⁻shunned by men,⁻ᵇ
A man of suffering, familiar with disease.
ᶜ⁻As one who hid his face from us,⁻ᶜ
He was despised, we held him of no account.
⁴Yet it was our sickness that he was bearing,
Our suffering that he endured.
We accounted him plagued,
Smitten and afflicted by God;
⁵But he was wounded because of our sins,

b   Cf. Ezra 1.7-8; 5.14-15
c   Heb "you"
d   Meaning of Heb uncertain

a-a   I.e. the vindication which the arm of the LORD effects
b-b   Meaning of Heb uncertain
c-c   I.e. as a leper; cf. Lev. 13.45 f.

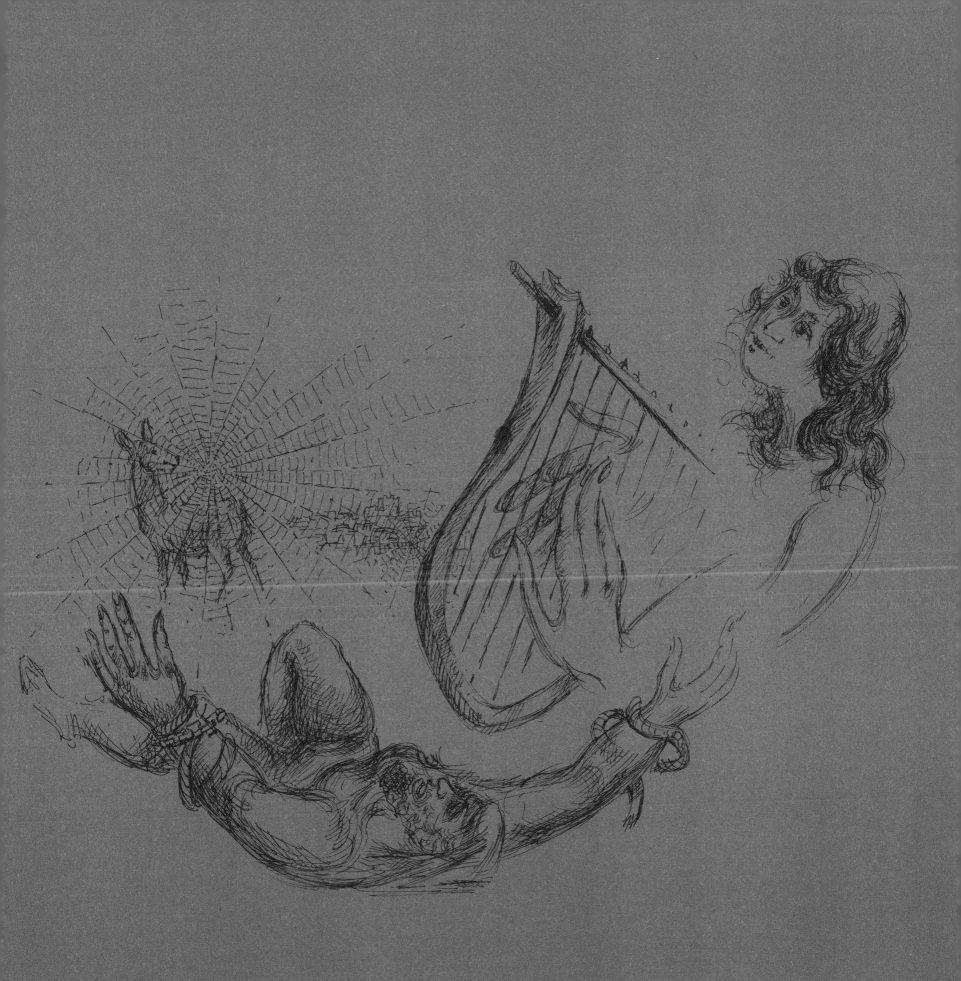

Crushed because of our iniquities.
He bore the chastisement that made us whole,
And by his bruises we were healed.
⁶We all went astray like sheep,
Each going his own way;
And the LORD visited upon him
The guilt of all of us.

⁷He was maltreated, yet he was submissive,
He did not open his mouth;
Like a sheep being led to slaughter,
Like a ewe, dumb before those who shear her,
He did not open his mouth.
⁸By oppressive judgment he was taken away,
ᵇ⁻Who could describe his abode?⁻ᵇ
For he was cut off from the land of the living
Through the sin of My people, who deserved the
    punishment.
⁹And his grave was set among the wicked,
ᵈ⁻And with the rich, in his death⁻ᵈ—
Though he had done no injustice
And had spoken no falsehood.
¹⁰But the LORD chose to crush him ᵇ⁻by disease,
    That, if he made himself an offering for guilt,⁻ᵇ
He might see offspringᵉ and have long life,
And that through him the LORD's purpose might
    prosper.
¹¹Out of his anguish he shall see it;ᶠ
He shall enjoy it to the full through his devo-
tion.ᵍ

d-d *Emendation yields "And his tomb with evildoers"*
e *Emendation yields "His arm," i.e. His vindication; cf. v. 1*
    with note
f *I.e. The arm of the Lord; see preceding note*
g *For this sense of da'ath see 11.2,9*

a-a *Lit. "Let the cloths of your dwelling extend"*
b *I.e. the foreigners who had occupied regions from which*
    Israelites had been exiled; cf. II Ki. 17.24

My righteous servant makes the many righteous,
    It is their punishment that he bears;
¹²Assuredly, I will give him the many as his portion,
He shall receive the multitude as his spoil.
For he exposed himself to death
And was numbered among the sinners,
Whereas he bore the guilt of the many
And made intercession for sinners.

54

¹Shout, O barren one,
You who bore no child!
Shout aloud for joy,
You who did not travail!
For the children of the wife forlorn
Shall outnumber those of the espoused
                    —said the LORD.
²Enlarge the site of your tent,
ᵃ⁻Extend the size of your dwelling,⁻ᵃ
Do not stint!
Lengthen the ropes, and drive the pegs firm.
³For you shall spread out to the right and the left;
Your offspring shall dispossess nationsᵇ
And shall people the desolate towns.

⁴Fear not, you shall not be shamed;
Do not cringe, you shall not be disgraced.
For you shall forget
The reproach of your youth,
And remember no more
The shame of your widowhood.
⁵For He who made you will espouse you—

His name is "Lord of Hosts";
The Holy One of Israel will redeem you,
Who is called "God of all the Earth."
⁶The Lord has called you back
As a wife forlorn and forsaken.
Can one cast off the wife of his youth?
                                —said your God.

⁷For a little while I forsook you,
But with vast love I will bring you back.
⁸In slight anger, for a moment,
I hid My face from you;
But with kindness everlasting
I will take you back in love
—Said the Lord your Redeemer.
⁹For this to Me is like the waters^c of Noah:
As I swore that the waters of Noah
Nevermore would flood the earth,
So I swear that I will not
Be angry with you or rebuke you.
¹⁰For the mountains may move
And the hills be shaken,
But my loyalty shall never move from you,
Nor My covenant of friendship be shaken
—Said the Lord, who takes you back in love,

¹¹Unhappy, storm-tossed one, uncomforted!
I will lay carbuncles^d as your building stones
And make your foundations of sapphires.
¹²I will make your battlements of rubies,
Your gates of precious stones,
The whole encircling wall of gems.
¹³And all your children shall be disciples of the
    Lord,
And great shall be the happiness of your children;
¹⁴You shall be established through righteousness.

You shall be safe from oppression,
And shall have no fear;
From ruin, and it shall not come near you.
¹⁵^eSurely no harm can be done
Without My consent:
Whoever would harm you
Shall fall because of you.
¹⁶It is I who created the smith
To fan the charcoal fire
And produce the tools for his work;
So it is I who create
The instruments of havoc.
¹⁷No weapon formed against you
Shall succeed,
And every tongue that contends with you at law
You shall defeat.
Such is the lot of the servants of the Lord,
Such their triumph through Me
                                —declares the Lord.

55

¹Ho, all who are thirsty,
Come for water,
Even if you have no money;
Come, buy food and eat:
Buy food without money,
Wine and milk without cost.
²Why do you spend money for what is not bread,
Your earnings for what does not satisfy?

---

c   Other Heb mss. and the ancient versions read "days"
d   Taking pukh as a by-form of nophekh; so already Rashi
e   Meaning of verse uncertain

Give heed to Me,
And you shall eat choice food
And enjoy the richest viands.
³Incline your ear and come to Me;
Hearken, and you shall be revived.
And I will make with you an everlasting cove-
nant,
The enduring loyalty promised to David.
⁴ᵃ⁻As I made him a leaderᵇ of peoples,
A prince and commander of peoples,
⁵So you shall summon a nation you did not know,
And a nation that did not know you
Shall come running to youᵃ—
For the sake of the Lᴏʀᴅ your God,
The Holy One of Israel who has glorified you.

⁶Seek the Lᴏʀᴅ while He can be found,
Call to Him while He is near.
⁷Let the wicked give up his ways,
The sinful man his plans;
Let him turn back to the Lᴏʀᴅ,
And He will pardon him;
To our God,
For he freely forgives.

For My plans are not your plans,
Nor are My waysᶜ your ways
—declares the Lᴏʀᴅ.
⁹But as the heavens are high above the earth,
So are My waysᶜ high above your waysᶜ
And My plans above your plans.

a-a *Cf. II Sam. 22.44-45// Ps. 18.44-45*
b *Cf. Targum; others "witness"*
c-c *Emendation yields "words"; cf. vv. 11 and 40.7*
d-d *Lit. "seed for the sower and bread for the eater"*
e *I.e. leave the Babylonian exile*

¹⁰For as the rain or snow drops from heaven
And returns not there,
But soaks the earth
And makes it bring forth vegetation,
Yielding ᵈ⁻seed for sowing and bread for eating,⁻ᵈ
¹¹So is the word that issues from My mouth:
It comes not back to Me its task undone,
But performs what I purpose,
Achieves what I sent it to do.
¹²Yea, you shall leaveᵉ in joy and be led home
secure.
Before you, mount and hill shall shout aloud,
And all the trees of the field shall clap their hands.
¹³Instead of the brier, a cypress shall rise;
Instead of the nettle, a myrtle shall rise.
These shall stand as a testimony to the Lᴏʀᴅ,
As an everlasting sign that shall not perish.

56

¹Thus said the Lᴏʀᴅ:
Observe what is right and do what is just;
For soon My salvation shall come,
And my deliverance be revealed.

²Happy is the man who does this,
The man who holds fast to it:
Who keeps the sabbath and does not profane it,
And stays his hand from doing any evil.

³Let not the foreigner say,
Who has attached himself to the Lᴏʀᴅ,
"The Lᴏʀᴅ will keep me apart from His people;"

And let not the eunuch say,
"I am a withered tree."
⁴For thus said the Lord:
"As regards the eunuchs who keep My sabbaths,
Who have chosen what I desire
And hold fast to My covenant—
⁵I will give them, in My House
And within My walls,
A monument and a name
Better than sons or daughters.
I will give them an everlasting name
Which shall not perish.
⁶As regards the foreigners who attach themselves
    to the Lord,
To minister to Him,
And to love the name of the Lord,
To be His servants—
All who keep the sabbath and do not profane it,
And who hold fast to My covenant—
⁷I will bring them to My sacred mount
And let them rejoice in My house of prayer.
Their burnt offerings and sacrifices
Shall be welcome on My altar;
For My House shall be called
A house of prayer for all peoples."
⁸Thus declares the Lord God,
Who gathers the dispersed of Israel:
"I will gather still more to those already
    gathered."

⁹All you wild beasts, come and devour,
All you beasts of the forest!
¹⁰The*ᵃ* watchmen are blind, all of them,
They know nothing.
They are all dumb dogs
That cannot bark;

They lie sprawling,*ᵇ*
They love to drowse.
¹¹Moreover, the dogs are greedy;
They never know satiety.
*ᶜ⋅*As for the shepherds, they know not
What it is to give heed.⁻*ᶜ*
Everyone has turned his own way,
Every last one seeks his own advantage.
¹²"Come, I'll buy some wine;
Let us swill liquor.
And tomorrow will be just the same,
Or even much grander!"

57

¹The righteous man perishes,
And no one takes it to heart;
Pious men are taken away,
And no one gives thought
That because of evil
The righteous was taken away.
²Yet he shall come to peace,
*ᵃ⋅*He shall have rest on his couch⁻*ᵃ*
Who walked straightforward.

³But as for you, come closer,
You sons of a sorceress,
You offspring of an adulterer and a harlot!*ᵇ*

a   *Heb "his"*
b   *Meaning of Heb uncertain*
c-c *Meaning of Heb uncertain. Emendation yields "Neither do*
      the shepherds ever know sufficiency." Cf. Prov. 30.15,16

a-a *Heb "They shall have rest on their couches"*
b   *Lit. "she acts the harlot"*

⁴With whom do you act so familiarly?
At whom do you open your mouth
And stick out your tongue?
Why, you are children of iniquity,
Offspring of treachery,
⁵You who inflame*c* yourselves
Among the terebinths,
Under every verdant tree;
Who slaughter children in the wadis,
Among*d* the clefts of the rocks.
⁶*e⁻*With such*f* are your share and portion,⁻*e*
They, they are your allotment;
To them you have poured out libations,
Presented offerings.
Should I relent in the face of this?
⁷On a high and lofty hill
You have set your couch;
There, too, you have gone up
To perform sacrifices.
⁸Behind the door and doorpost
You have directed your thoughts,
*e⁻*Abandoning Me, you have gone up
On the couch you made so wide.
You have made a covenant with them,*f*
You have loved bedding with them;*g*
You have chosen lust.*h*

⁹You have approached⁻*e* the king*i* with oil,
You have provided many perfumes.
And you have sent your envoys afar,
Even down to the nether world.*j*
¹⁰Though wearied by much travel,
You never said, "I give up!"
You found gratification for your lust,
And so you never wearied.
¹¹*k⁻*Whom do you dread and fear,
That you tell lies?⁻*k*
But you gave no thought to Me,
You paid no heed.
It is because I have stood idly by *l⁻*so long⁻*l*
That you have no fear of Me.
¹²I hereby pronounce *m⁻*judgment upon your
deeds:⁻*m*
*n⁻*Your assorted [idols]⁻*n* shall not avail you,
¹³Shall not save you when you cry out.
They shall all be borne off by the wind,
Snatched away by a breeze.
But those who trust in Me shall inherit the land
And possess My holy mountain.

¹⁴[The Lord] says:
Build up, build up a highway!
Clear a road!
Remove all obstacles
From the road of My people!
¹⁵For thus said He who high aloft
Forever dwells, whose Name is Holy:
I dwell on high, in holiness;
Yet with the contrite and the lowly in spirit—
Reviving the spirits of the lowly,
Reviving the hearts of the contrite.
¹⁶For I will not always contend,
I will not be angry forever:

c   *I.e. in some frenzied idolatrous rite*
d   *Heb "under"*
e-e   *Meaning of Heb uncertain*
f   *The cult-trees referred to above in v. 5*
g   *I.e. with the objects of worship mentioned above*
h   *Like Ugaritic yd, from root ydd (cf. Deut. 33.12)*
i   *Or "Moloch"*
j   *I.e. you have brought tribute to alien cults as to a king*
k-k *Emendation yields*
          "Them you dreaded and feared,
            And so you gave them thought,"
l-l   *Emendation yields "and shut My eyes"*
m-m *Lit. "your retribution and your deeds"*
n-n   *Brought up from v. 13 for clarity*

Nay, I *e-*who make spirits flag,*-e*
Also create the breath of life.
¹⁷For his*o* sinful greed I was angry;
I struck him and turned away in My wrath.
*p-*Though stubborn he follows the way of his
heart,*-p*
¹⁸I note how he fares and will heal him:
I will guide him and mete out solace to him,
And to the mourners within him
¹⁹   heartening,*q* comforting*r* words:
It shall be well,
Well with the far and the near
                    —said the LORD—
And I will heal him.
²⁰But the wicked are like the troubled sea
Which cannot rest,
Whose waters toss up mire and mud.
²¹There is no safety
                    —said my God—
                              for the wicked.

58

¹Cry with full throat, without restraint;
Raise your voice like a ram's horn!
Declare to My people their transgression,
To the House of Jacob their sin.

²To be sure, they seek Me daily,
Eager to learn My ways.
Like a nation that does what is right,
That has not abandoned the laws of its God,
They ask Me for the right way,

They are eager for the nearness of God:
³"Why, when we fasted, did You not see;
When we starved our bodies, did You pay no
heed?"
Because on your fast day
You see to your business
And oppress all your laborers!
⁴Because you fast in strife and contention,
And you strike with a wicked fist!
Your fasting today is not such
As to make your voice heard on high.
⁵Is such the fast I desire,
A day for men to starve their bodies?
Is it bowing the head like a bulrush
And lying in sackcloth and ashes?
Do you call that a fast,
A day when the LORD is favorable?
⁶No, this is the fast I desire:
To unlock fetters of wickedness,
And untie the cords of the yoke*a*
To let the oppressed go free;
To break off every yoke.
⁷It is to share your bread with the hungry,
And to take the wretched poor into your home;
When you see the naked, to clothe him,
And not to ignore your own kin.

⁸Then shall your light burst through like the dawn
And your healing spring up quickly;
Your Vindicator shall march before you,

o   *I.e. Israel's*
p-p *Meaning of Heb uncertain. Emendation yields "When he
     has walked broken in the contrition of his heart,"*
q   *Lit. "the vigor of"; cf. Eccl. 12.1 and postbiblical* bori
r   *The Heb* nib *is otherwise unknown; its meaning is inferred
     from that of* nid *(cf. the verb* nad *"to condole") in the
     parallel expression in Job 16.5*

a   *Change of vocalization yields "lawlessness"; cf.* muṭṭeh,
     Ezek. 9.9

The Presence of the LORD shall be your rear
   guard.
⁹Then, when you call, The LORD will answer;
  When you cry, He will say: Here I am.
  If you banish the yoke*ᵃ* from your midst,
  *ᵇ·*The menacing hand,*·ᵇ* and evil speech,
¹⁰And you offer your compassion*ᶜ* to the hungry
  And satisfy the famished creature—
  Then shall your light shine in darkness,
  And your gloom shall be like noonday.
¹¹The LORD will guide you always;
  He will slake your thirst in drought*ᵈ*
  And give strength to your bones.
  You shall be like a watered garden,
  Like a spring whose waters do not fail.
¹²Men from your midst shall rebuild ancient ruins,
  You shall restore foundations laid long ago.
  And you shall be called
  "Repairer of fallen walls,
  Restorer of lanes for habitation."
¹³If you *ᵉ·*refrain from trampling*·ᵉ* the sabbath,
  From pursuing your affairs on My holy day;
  If you call the sabbath "delight,"
  The LORD's holy day "honored;"
  And if you honor it and go not your ways
  Nor look to your affairs, nor strike bargains—
¹⁴Then you *ᶠ·*can seek the favor of the LORD.*·ᶠ*
  I will set you astride the heights of the earth,
  And let you enjoy the heritage of your father
   Jacob—
  For the mouth of the LORD has spoken.

b-b *Lit. "Extending the finger"*
c   *Some Heb mss. and ancient versions read "bread"*
d   *Meaning of Heb uncertain*
e-e *Lit. "turn back your foot from"*
f-f *Cf. Ps. 37.4; Job 22.26-27; 27.10*

a   *Or "blood"*

59

¹No, the LORD's hand is not too short to save,
  Or His ear too dull to hear;
²But your iniquities have been a barrier
  Between you and your God,
  Your sins have made Him turn His face away
  And refuse to hear you.
³For your hands are defiled with crime*ᵃ*
  And your fingers with iniquity.
  Your lips speak falsehood,
  Your tongue utters treachery.
⁴No one sues justly
  Or pleads honestly;
  They rely on emptiness and speak falsehood,
  Conceiving wrong and begetting evil.

⁵They hatch adder's eggs
  And weave spider webs;
  He who eats of those eggs will die,
  And if one is crushed, it hatches out a viper.
⁶Their webs will not serve as a garment,
  What they make cannot serve as clothing;
  Their deeds are deeds of mischief,
  Their hands commit lawless acts,
⁷Their feet run after evil,
  They hasten to shed the blood of the innocent.
  Their plans are plans of mischief,
  Destructiveness and injury are on their roads.
⁸They do not care for the way of integrity,
  There is no justice on their paths.
  They make their courses crooked,
  No one who walks in them cares for integrity.

⁹That is why redress is far from us,

And vindication does not reach us.
We hope for light, and lo! there is darkness;
For a gleam, and we must walk in gloom.
¹⁰We grope, like blind men along a wall;
Like those without eyes we grope.
We stumble at noon, as if in darkness;
ᵇ⁻Among the sturdy, we are⁻ᵇ like the dead.
¹¹We all growl like bears
And moan like doves.
We hope for redress, and there is none;
For victory, and it is far from us.
¹²For our many sins are before You,
Our guilt testifies against us.
We are aware of our sins,
And we know well our iniquities:
¹³Rebellion, faithlessness to the LORD,
And turning away from our God,
Planning fraud and treachery,
Conceiving ͨ lies and uttering them with the
throat.ᵈ
¹⁴And so redress is turned back
And vindication stays afar,
Because honesty stumbles in the public square
And uprightness cannot enter.
¹⁵Honesty has been lacking,
He who turns away from evil is despoiled.

The LORD saw and was displeased
That there was no redress.
¹⁶He saw that there was no man,
He gazed long, but no one intervened.
Then His own arm won Him triumph,
His victorious right hand ͤ supported Him.
¹⁷He donned victory like a coat of mail,
With a helmet of triumph on His head;
He clothed Himself with garments of retribution,

Wrapped himself in zeal as in a robe.
¹⁸ᶠ⁻According to their deserts, so shall He repay⁻ᶠ
Fury to His foes, make requital to His enemies;
He shall make requital to the distant lands.
¹⁹From the west they shall revere ͡ the LORD Him-
self,ʰ
And from the east His Presence.
For He shall come like a hemmed-in stream
Which the wind of the LORD drives on;
²⁰He shall come as redeemer to Zion,
To those in Jacob who turn back from sin
—declares the LORD.

²¹ And this shall be My covenant with them, said
the LORD: My spirit ͥ which is upon you, and the
words which I have placed in your mouth shall
not be absent from your mouth, nor from the
mouth of your children, nor from the mouth of
your children's children—said the LORD—from
now on, for all time.ʲ

60

¹Arise, shine, for your light has dawned;
The Presence of the LORD has shone upon you!
²Behold! Darkness shall cover the earth,
And thick clouds the peoples;

b-b *Meaning of Heb uncertain. Emendation yields "in the day-*
time, . . ."
c *One ancient Heb ms. (1QIsᵃ) lacks this word*
d *Lit. "heart"; see note at 33.18 and frequently elsewhere*
e *Cf. Ps. 98.1-2*
f-f *Meaning of Heb uncertain*
g *Or (with a number of mss. and editions) "see"*
h *Lit. "the name of the LORD"*
i *I.e. the gift of prophecy; cf., e.g., 61.1*
j *Israel is to be a prophet-nation; cf. 51.16*

But upon you the LORD will shine,
  And His Presence be seen over you.
³And nations shall walk by your light,
  Kings, by your shining radiance.

⁴Raise your eyes and look about:
  They have all gathered and come to you.
  Your sons shall be brought from afar,
  Your daughters like babes on shoulders.
⁵As you behold, you will glow;
  Your heart will throb and thrill—
  For the wealth of the seaᵃ shall pass on to you,
  The riches of nations shall flow to you.
⁶Dust clouds of camels shall cover you,
  Dromedaries of Midian and Ephah.
  They all shall come from Sheba;
  They shall bear gold and frankincense,
  And shall herald the glories of the LORD.
⁷All the flocks of Kedar shall be assembled for you,
  The rams of Nebaioth shall serve your needs;
  They shall be welcome offerings on My altar,
  And I will add glory to My glorious House.

⁸Who are these that float like a cloud,
  Like doves to their cotes?
⁹ᵇ⁻Behold, the coastlands await me,⁻ᵇ
  With Tarshish-ships in the lead,
  To bring your sons from afar,
  And theirᶜ silver and gold as well—
  For the name of the LORD your God,
  For the Holy One of Israel, who has glorified
    you.

a Emendation yields "coastlands"
b-b Emendation yields "The vessels of the coastlands are gather-
    ing"
c I.e. of the people of the coastlands
d Lit. "breasts of kings" or "breasts of kingdoms"

¹⁰Aliens shall rebuild your walls,
  Their kings shall wait upon you—
  For in anger I struck you down,
  But in favor I take you back.
¹¹Your gates shall always stay open—
  Day and night they shall never be shut—
  To let in the wealth of the nations,
  With their kings in procession.

¹²For the nation or the kingdom
  That does not serve you shall perish;
  Such nations shall be destroyed.

¹³The majesty of Lebanon shall come to you—
  Cypress and pine and box—
  To adorn the site of My Sanctuary,
  To glorify the place where My feet rest.

¹⁴Bowing before you, shall come
  The children of those who tormented you;
  Prostrate at the soles of your feet
  Shall be all those who reviled you;
  And you shall be called
  "City of the LORD,
  Zion of the Holy One of Israel."
¹⁵Whereas you have been forsaken,
  Rejected, with none passing through,
  I will make you a pride everlasting,
  A joy for age after age.
¹⁶You shall suck the milk of the nations,
  Suckle at royal breasts.ᵈ
  And you shall know
  That I the LORD am your Savior,
  I, The Mighty One of Jacob, am your Redeemer.

¹⁷Instead of copper I will bring gold,

I will pay them their wages faithfully,
And make a covenant with them for all time.
⁹Their offspring shall be known among the nations,
Their descendants in the midst of the peoples.
All who see them shall recognize
That they are a stock the LORD has blessed.

¹⁰I greatly rejoice in the LORD,
My whole being exults in my God.
For He has clothed me with garments of triumph,
Wrapped me in a robe of victory,
Like a bridegroom adorned with a turban,
Like a bride bedecked with her finery.
¹¹For as the earth brings forth her growth
And a garden makes the seed shoot up,
So the Lord GOD will make
Victory and renown shoot up
In the presence of all the nations.

62

¹For the sake of Zion I will not be silent,
For the sake of Jerusalem I will not be still,
Till her victory emerge resplendent
And her triumph like a flaming torch.
²Nations shall see your victory,
And every king your majesty;
And you shall be called by a new name
Which the LORD Himself shall bestow.

a-a *Change of vocalization yields "He who rebuilds you"*
b *I.e. those who are to remind the Lord about Jerusalem*

³You shall be a glorious crown
In the hand of the LORD,
And a royal diadem
In the palm of your God.

⁴Nevermore shall you be called "Forsaken,"
Nor shall your land be called "Desolate";
But you shall be called "I delight in her,"
And your land "Espoused."
For the LORD takes delight in you,
And your land shall be espoused.
⁵As a youth espouses a maiden,
ᵃ‧Your sonsᵃ shall espouse you;
And as a bridegroom rejoices over his bride,
So will your God rejoice over you.

⁶Upon your walls, O Jerusalem,
I have set watchmen,
Who shall never be silent
By day or by night.
O you, the LORD's remembrancers,ᵇ
Take no rest.
⁷And give no rest to Him,
Until He establish Jerusalem
And make her renowned on earth.

⁸The LORD has sworn by His right hand,
By His mighty arm:
Nevermore will I give your new grain
To your enemies for food,
Nor shall foreigners drink the new wine
For which you have labored.
⁹But those who harvest it shall eat it
And give praise to the LORD;
And those who gather it shall drink it
In My sacred courts.

¹⁰Pass through, pass through the gates!
  Clear the road for the people;
  Build up, build up the highway,
  Remove the rocks!
  Raise an ensign over the peoples!
¹¹See, the LORD has proclaimed
  To the end of the earth:
  Announce to Fair Zion,
  Your Deliverer is coming!
  See, his reward is with Him,
  His recompense before Him.^c
¹²And they shall be called, "The Holy People,
  The Redeemed of the LORD,"
  And you shall be called, "Sought Out,
  A City Not Forsaken."

63

¹Who is this coming from Edom,
  In crimsoned garments from Bozrah—
  Who is this, majestic in attire,
  ^{a-}Pressing forward^{-a} in His great might?
  "It is I, who contend victoriously,
  Powerful^b to give triumph."

²Why is your clothing so red,
  Your garments like his who treads grapes?^c
³"I trod out a vintage alone;
  ^{d-}Of the peoples^{-d} no man was with Me.
  I trod them down in My anger,
  Trampled them in My rage;
  Their life-blood^e bespattered My garments,
  And all My clothing was stained.

⁴For I had planned a day of vengeance,
  And My year of redemption arrived.
⁵Then I looked, but there was none to help;
  I stared, but there was none to aid—
  So My own arm wrought the triumph,
  And ^{f-}My own rage^{-f} was My aid.
⁶I trampled peoples in My anger,
  ^{g-}I made them drunk with^{-g} My rage,
  And I hurled their glory to the ground."

⁷I will recount the kind acts of the LORD,
  The praises of the LORD—
  For all that the LORD has wrought for us,
  The vast bounty to the House of Israel
  That He bestowed upon them
  According to His mercy and His great kindness.
⁸He thought: Surely they are My people,
  Children who will not play false.
  ^{h-}So He was their Deliverer.
⁹In all their troubles He was troubled,
  And the angel of His Presence delivered them.^{-h}
  In His love and pity
  He Himself redeemed them,
  Raised them, and exalted them
  All the days of old.
¹⁰But they rebelled, and grieved
  His holy spirit;

c   See note at 40.10

a-a *Meaning of Heb uncertain; emendation yields "striding"*
b   *Change of vocalization yields "contest triumphantly"; cf.*
       19.20
c   *Lit. "in a press"*
d-d *Emendation yields "Peoples, and"*
e   *Meaning of Heb uncertain*
f-f *Many mss. read weṣidqathi "My victorious [right hand]";*
       cf. 59.16
g-g *Many mss. and Targum read "I shattered them in"; cf. 14.25*
h-h *Ancient versions read "So He was their Deliverer*
         9 In all their troubles.
           No [so Kethib] angel or messenger,
           His own Presence delivered them,"

Then He became their enemy,
And Himself made war against them.
¹¹Then theyⁱ remembered the ancient days,
^{j-}Him, who pulled His people^{-j} out [of the
water]:
"Where is He who brought them up from the
Sea
Along with the shepherd^k of His flock?
Where is He who put
In their^l midst His holy spirit,
¹²Who made His glorious arm
March at the right hand of Moses,
Who divided the waters before them
To make Himself a name for all time,
¹³Who led them through the deeps
So that they did not stumble—
As a horse in a desert,
¹⁴Like a beast descending to the plain?"
'Twas the spirit of the LORD ^{m-}gave them rest;^{-m}
Thus did You shepherd Your people
To win for Yourself a glorious name.

¹⁵Look down from heaven and see,
From Your holy and glorious height!
Where is Your zeal, Your power?
Your yearning and Your love
Are being withheld from us!ⁿ
¹⁶Surely You are our Father:

Though Abraham regard us not,
And Israel recognize us not,
You, O LORD, are our Father;
From of old, Your name is "Our Redeemer."
¹⁷Why, LORD, do You make us stray from Your
ways,
And turn our hearts away from revering You?
Relent for the sake of Your servants,
The tribes that are Your very own!
¹⁸Our foes have trampled Your Sanctuary,
Which Your holy people ^{o-}possessed but a little
while.^{-o}
¹⁹We have become as a people You never ruled,
To which Your name was never attached.

If You would but tear open the heavens and come
down,
So that mountains would quake before You—

64

^{1a}As when fire kindles brushwood,
And fire makes water boil—
So that nations may tremble at Your Presence,
²When You do wonders we dared not hope for
(When You come down
And mountains quake before You),
³Which were never heard or noted.
Which no eye has seen, O God, but You
Who act for those who hope in You!^b
⁴You have struck him who would gladly do
justice,
And remember You in Your ways.

---

i   Heb "he"
j-j Heb moshe 'ammo, a play on the name Moshe (Moses)
k   So many mss. and ancient versions; other texts "shepherds"
l   Or "his"
m-m Emendation yields "guided them"
n   Heb "me." Emendation yields
         "[Where are] Your yearning and Your love?
         Let them not be restrained!"
o-o Meaning of Heb uncertain

a   Meaning of vv. 1-4 uncertain
b   Heb "Him"

It is because You are angry that we have sinned;
c-We have been steeped in them from of old,
And can we be saved?-*c*
⁵We have all become like an unclean thing,
And all our virtues like a filthy rag.
We are all withering like leaves,
And our iniquities, like a wind, carry us off.
⁶Yet no one invokes Your name,
Rouses himself to cling to You.
For You have hidden Your face from us,
And *d*-made us melt because of-*d* our iniquities.
⁷But now, O Lord, You are our Father;
We are the clay, and You are the Potter,
We are all the work of Your hands.
⁸Be not so very angry, O Lord,
Do not remember iniquity forever.
Oh, look down to Your people, to us all!
⁹Your holy cities have become a desert:
Zion has become a desert,
Jerusalem a desolation.
¹⁰Our holy Temple, our pride,
Where our fathers praised You,
Has been consumed by fire:
And all that was dear to us is ruined.
¹¹At such things will You restrain Yourself, O
Lord,
Will You stand idly by and let us suffer so
heavily?

65

¹I responded to*ᵃ* those who did not ask,
I was at hand to those who did not seek Me;

I said, "Here I am, here I am,"
To a nation that did not invoke My name.
²I constantly spread out My hands
To a disobedient people,
Who walk the way that is not good,
Following their own designs;
³The people who provoke My anger,
Who continually, to My very face,
Sacrifice in gardens and burn incense on tiles;
⁴Who sit inside tombs
And pass the night in secret places;
Who eat the flesh of swine
And have broth of unclean things in their bowls;
⁵Who say, "Keep your distance! Don't come
closer!
b-For I would render you consecrated."-*b*
Such things make My anger rage,
Like fire blazing all day long.
⁶See, this is recorded before Me;
I will not stand idly by, but will repay,
Deliver *c*-their*d* sins-*c* into their bosom,
⁷And the sins of their fathers as well

            —said the Lord—

For they made offerings upon the mountains
And affronted Me upon the hills.
I will count out their recompense in full,*ᵉ*
Into their bosoms.
⁸Thus said the Lord:
As, when new wine is present in the cluster,

c-c *Emendation yields "Because You have hidden Yourself we*
    have offended." For the thought cf. 63.17
d-d *Emendation yields "delivered us into the power of"*

a   *Lit. "I let Myself be inquired of"*
b-b *Taking* qedashtikha *as equivalent to* qiddashtikha; *others*
    "For I am holier than thou"; cf. Ezek. 49.19
c-c *Brought up from v. 7 for clarity*
d   *Heb "your"*
e   *Taking* rishonah *as equivalent to* beroshah; *cf. Lev. 5.24*
    Meaning of Heb uncertain

One says, "Don't destroy it; there's good in it,"
So will I do for the sake of My servants,
And not destroy everything.
⁹I will bring forth offspring from Jacob,
From Judah heirs to My mountains;
My chosen ones shall take possession,
My servants shall dwell thereon.
¹⁰Sharon*ᶠ* shall become a pasture for flocks,
And the Valley of Achor a place for cattle to lie
down,
For My people who seek Me.

¹¹But as for you who forsake the Lord,
Who ignore My holy mountain,
Who set a table for Luck*ᵍ*
And pour mixed wine for Destiny*ᵍ*:
¹²I will destine you for the sword,
You will all kneel down, to be slaughtered—
Because, when I called, you did not answer,
When I spoke, you would not listen.
You did what I hold evil,
And chose what I do not want.

¹³Assuredly thus said the Lord God:
My servants shall eat, and you shall hunger;
My servants shall drink, and you shall thirst;
My servants shall rejoice, and you shall be shamed;
¹⁴My servants shall shout in gladness,
And you shall cry out in anguish,
Howling in heartbreak.
¹⁵You shall leave behind a name
By which My chosen ones shall curse:

"So may the Lord God slay you!"
But His servants shall be given a *ʰ*different
name.*ʰ*
¹⁶For whoever blesses himself in the land
Shall bless himself by the true God;
And whoever swears in the land
Shall swear by the true God.
The former troubles shall be forgotten,
Shall be hidden from My eyes.

¹⁷For behold! I am creating
A new heaven and a new earth;
The former things shall not be remembered,
They shall never come to mind.
¹⁸Be glad, then, and rejoice forever
In what I am creating.
For I shall create Jerusalem as a joy,
And her people as a delight;
¹⁹And I will rejoice in Jerusalem
And delight in her people.
Never again shall be heard there
The sounds of weeping and wailing.
²⁰No more shall there be an infant or graybeard
Who does not live out his days.
He who dies at a hundred years
Shall be reckoned a youth,
And he who fails to reach a hundred
Shall be reckoned accursed.
²¹They shall build houses and dwell in them,
They shall plant vineyards and enjoy their fruit.
²²They shall not build for others to dwell in,
Or plant for others to enjoy.
For the days of My people shall be
As long as the days of a tree,
My chosen ones shall outlive*ⁱ*
The work of their hands.

f   *Emendation yields "Jeshimon," the bleak southeast corner*
      of the Jordan Valley; cf. Nu. 21.20; 23.8
g   *Names of heathen deities*
h-h *I.e. a name to be used in blessing*
i   *Lit. "wear out"*

²³They shall not toil to no purpose;
They shall not bear children ^{j-}for terror;^{-j}
But they shall be a people blessed by the Lord,
And their offspring shall remain with them.
²⁴Before they pray, I will answer;
While they are still speaking, I will respond.
²⁵The wolf and the lamb shall graze together,
And the lion shall eat straw like the ox,
And the serpent's food shall be earth.
²⁶In all My sacred mount^k
Nothing evil or vile shall be done
      —said the Lord.

66

¹Thus said the Lord:
The heaven is My throne
And the earth is My footstool:
Where could you build a house for Me,
What place could serve as My abode?
²All this was made by My hand,
And thus it all came into being
    —declares the Lord.
Yet to such a one I look:
To the poor and broken-hearted,
Who is concerned about My word.

^{3a}They who slaughter oxen and slay humans,
Who sacrifice sheep and immolate^b dogs,
Who present as oblation the blood of swine,
Who offer^c incense and worship false gods—
Just as they have chosen their ways

And take pleasure in their abominations,
⁴So will I choose to mock them,
To bring on them the very thing they dread.
For I called and none responded,
I spoke and none paid heed.
They did what I deem evil
And chose what I do not want.

⁵Hear the word of the Lord,
You who are concerned about His word!
Your kinsmen who hate you,
Who spurn you because of Me,^d are saying,
"Let the Lord manifest His Presence,
So that we may look upon your joy."
But theirs shall be the shame.
⁶Hark, tumult from the city,
Thunder from the Temple!
It is the thunder of the Lord
As He deals retribution to His foes.

⁷Before she labored, she was delivered;
Before her pangs came, she bore a son.
⁸Who ever heard the like?
Who ever witnessed such events?
Can a land pass through travail
In a single day?
Or is a nation born
All at once?
Yet Zion travailed
And at once bore her children!

j-j *Emendation yields "in vain"*
k *See note at 11.9*

a *Vv. 3-4 refer to practioners of idolatrous rites; cf. v. 17 and Isa. 57.5-8; 65.1-12*
b *Lit. "break the necks of"*
c *Heb* mazkir, *refers to giving the "token portion"* ('azkarah); *cf. Lev. 2.2, etc.*
d *Lit. "My name"*

⁹Shall I who bring on labor not bring about birth?
                    —says the Lord.
Shall I who cause birth shut the womb?
                    —said your God.
¹⁰Rejoice with Jerusalem and be glad for her,
  All you who love her!
  Join in her jubilation,
  All you who mourned over her—
¹¹That you may suck from her breast
  Consolation to the full,
  That you may draw from her bosom*e*
  Glory to your delight.

¹²For thus said the Lord:
  I will extend to her
  Prosperity like a stream,
  The wealth of nations
  Like a wadi in flood;
  And you shall drink of it.
  You shall be carried on shoulders
  And dandled upon knees.
¹³As a mother comforts her son
  So I will comfort you;
  You shall find comfort in Jerusalem.
¹⁴You shall see and your heart shall rejoice,
  Your limbs shall flourish like grass.
  The power of the Lord shall be revealed
  In behalf of His servants;
  But He shall rage against His foes.

¹⁵See, the Lord is coming with fire—
  His chariots are like a whirlwind—

To vent His anger in fury,
  His rebuke in flaming fire.
¹⁶For with fire will the Lord contend,
  With His sword, against all flesh;
  And many shall be the slain of the Lord.

¹⁷ Those who sanctify and purify themselves to enter the groves, *f-*imitating one in the center,*-f* eating the flesh of the swine, the reptile, and the mouse, shall one and all come to an end—declares the Lord. ¹⁸*g*For I [know] their deeds and purposes.

[The time] has come to gather all the nations and tongues; they shall come and behold My glory. ¹⁹I will set a sign among them, and send from them survivors to the nations: to Tarshish, Pul, and Lud—that draw the bow—to Tubal, Javan, and the distant coasts, that have never heard My fame nor beheld My glory. They shall declare My glory among these nations. ²⁰And out of all the nations, said the Lord, they shall bring all your brothers on horses, in chariots and drays, on mules and dromedaries, to Jerusalem My holy mountain as an offering to the Lord—just as the Israelites bring an offering in a pure vessel to the House of the Lord. ²¹And from them likewise I will take some to be *h-*levitical priests,*-h* said the Lord.
²²For as the new heaven and the new earth
  Which I will make
  Shall endure by My will
                    —declares the Lord—
  So shall your seed and your name endure.
²³And new moon after new moon,
  And sabbath after sabbath,

e   Meaning of Heb uncertain; others "abundance"
f-f Meaning of Heb uncertain
g   Exact construction of this verse uncertain; for the insertions
       in brackets, cf. Kimhi
h-h Some Heb mss. read "priests and Levites"

All flesh shall come to worship Me
                    —said the LORD.
²⁴They shall go out and gaze
  On the corpses of the men who rebelled against
    Me:
  Their worms shall not die,
  Nor their fire be quenched;
  They shall be a horror
  To all flesh.

        And new moon after new moon,
        And Sabbath after Sabbath,
        All flesh shall come to worship Me
                    —said the LORD.